"*The Interpersonal Problems Workbook* is a brilliant resource for anyone struggling with a pattern of relationship problems. It is straightforward, thoroughly researched, and wonderfully compassionate. This book is a gentle but powerful guide to becoming the person you want to be, and creating the relationships you want to have."

—**Shawn T. Smith, PsyD**, author of *The User's Guide to the Human Mind*

"Our relationships with others that provide such enrichment and meaning to our lives, can, unfortunately, also a serve as a source of deep pain and suffering. This scientifically-supported and easy-to-follow workbook provides a step-by-step way to break out of long-standing patterns of behavior that prevent our relationships from being more vital and fulfilling. Think of it as an operating manual for turning around troubled interpersonal relationships. I recommend this latest contribution by McKay and his colleagues not only as a self-help guidebook, but also as a useful adjunct to their related book for mental health professionals working with those who struggle with interpersonal relationship issues."

—**Robert Zettle**, author of *ACT for Depression*

"*The Interpersonal Problems Workbook* validates the emotional pain connected to interpersonal difficulties that we all experience throughout our lives. It provides worksheets and exercises to help readers gain insight into where this pain comes from, and teaches techniques to help people end these unhealthy patterns, subsequently having the effect of reducing emotional pain. This is a fabulous book that will help people get unstuck from ineffective relationship patterns, and that will provide clinicians with the much-needed, concrete tools to help clients with these issues."

—**Sheri Van Dijk, MSW, RSW**, psychotherapist and author of several books, including *Don't Let Your Emotions Run Your Life for Teens, Calming the Emotional Storm,* and *DBT Made Simple*

"*The Interpersonal Problems Workbook* is an excellent resource for any individual or therapist working with clients who have maladaptive relationship patterns. This workbook uses a treatment protocol that is grounded in the core principles of acceptance and commitment therapy. Not only do clients get to explore their schemas, but they get to learn about their core values and how to live a life of mindfulness. I highly recommend this book to anyone struggling with painful interpersonal problems. This workbook is an invaluable tool for any mental health practitioner or person wanting to improve his or her relationships."

—**Raychelle Cassada Lohmann, MS, LPC**, professional counselor, author of *The Anger Workbook for Teens, Staying Cool...When You're Steaming Mad,* and coauthor of *The Bullying Workbook for Teens*

"A well-conceived, research-based, step-by-step series of exercises guides individuals to identify and mindfully address the schemas that inhibit their ability to form happy, healthy relationships. It is not necessary to be especially well-versed in ACT to benefit from this practical approach. Everything you need to begin addressing the pain that accompanies poor interpersonal relating can be found in this highly worthwhile workbook."

—**Stan Tatkin, PsyD, MFT**, clinician, researcher, teacher, and developer of a Psychobiological Approach to Couple Therapy® (PACT)

"If you're tired of merely thinking and talking about your problems with family, loved ones, friends, colleagues, and coworkers, then this book is for you. It teaches you a host of new valuable skills that will actually not only help you with interpersonal problems but will also come in handy in many other areas of your life. The book explains in simple, straight-forward, and accessible language how certain thought patterns and beliefs about yourself and your relationship with the world can keep you unhappy and stuck in patterns of behavior that clearly have not worked in the past. It then quickly moves on and provides you with a variety of extremely helpful exercises that you can put into practice right away. These exercises are simple but they are not simplistic. They have proven themselves many times over and are backed up by a stack of research studies attesting to their usefulness. This book is for you and will help you if you are serious about moving past your relationship pain (and what your mind tells you about that pain) and are willing to take the steps toward doing what matters—you have nothing to lose and much to win!"

—**Georg Eifert, PhD**, Chapman University Professor Emeritus of Psychology and coauthor of the *Mindfulness and Acceptance Workbook for Anxiety*

"At the heart of happiness is the ability to have strong and healthy relationships. Struggling with interpersonal problems can make you miserable. This book teaches you proven techniques for developing the skills to relate to other people in a much healthier and productive manner. *The Interpersonal Problems Workbook* will help you deal with the thoughts and emotions that create obstacles in your relationships while also guiding you towards building genuine connections with the people in your life."

—**D. J. Moran**, founder of the MidAmerican Psychological Institute

"Inspired in part by the work of Jeffrey Young, founder of the schema therapy approach, *The Interpersonal Problems Workbook* offers valuable strategies for dealing with some of the most difficult challenges we face with some of the most important people in our lives. This comprehensive workbook provides the reader with meaningful ways to look beneath the trappings of early life themes that can prompt our self-defeating responses when triggered. We learn how to move beyond these embedded automatic patterns in order to achieve effective/adaptive interpersonal experiences and coping styles. Hats off to the authors for this creative and thoughtful guide."

—**Wendy Behary**, author of *Disarming the Narcissist*

"For most of us, when our relationships are not working, life is not working.
Despite their central link to human health and happiness, psychology has been appallingly lax in developing specific methods that will help with interpersonal problems. This book helps end that odd silence. It puts forward a creative, step-by-step approach that research suggests can make a real difference in the quality of your relationships, now. Its clear, sound guidance will help you create a better life for you and those you love. Highly recommended."

—**Steven C. Hayes**, cofounder of acceptance and commitment therapy and author of *Get Out of Your Mind and Into Your Life*

"*The Interpersonal Problems Skills Workbook* is a highly needed self-help book for those struggling with chronic interpersonal problems. The authors did an outstanding job guiding readers through the process of identifying their schemas, triggers as well as old behaviors; furthermore, they make sure to walk readers step-by-step on how to develop new behaviors that are in alignment with their interpersonal values. This self-help book will help everyone struggling with ongoing relationship problems. I highly recommend it not only because of its rich content but also because of the research that supports its evidence."

—**Patricia E. Zurita Ona, PsyD**, psychologist at the East Bay Behavior Therapy Center and coauthor of *Mind & Emotions*

"Reader, you are holding in your hands a resource that can profoundly improve and transform your interpersonal relationships. An entirely new approach to healing, this clear, brilliantly conceived workbook unites the ancient wisdom found in mindfulness practices with the practical skills of contemporary psychotherapy. Don't let a chance like this slip out of your hands."

—**Steve Flowers, MFT**, author of *The Mindful Path Through Shyness* and *Living With Your Heart Wide Open*

# THE
# Interpersonal
# Problems
# WORKBOOK

## ACT *to* End Painful Relationship Patterns

**MATTHEW McKAY, PhD**
**PATRICK FANNING**
**AVIGAIL LEV, PsyD**
**MICHELLE SKEEN, PsyD**

New Harbinger Publications, Inc.

## Publisher's Note

NEW HARBINGER PUBLICATIONS is a registered trademark of New Harbinger Publications, Inc.

Distributed in Canada by Raincoast Books

Copyright © 2013 by Matthew McKay, Patrick Fanning, Avigail Lev, and Michelle L. Skeen
New Harbinger Publications, Inc.
5674 Shattuck Avenue
Oakland, CA 94609
www.newharbinger.com

Cover design by Amy Shoup

Text design by Michele Waters-Kermes

Acquired by Jess O'Brien

Edited by Nelda Street

## Library of Congress Cataloging-in-Publication Data

McKay, Matthew.
  The interpersonal problems workbook : act to end painful relationship patterns / Matthew McKay, PhD, Patrick Fanning, Avigail Lev, PsyD, and Michelle Skeen, PsyD.
    pages cm
  Includes bibliographical references.
  ISBN 978-1-60882-836-4 (pbk. : alk. paper) -- ISBN 978-1-60882-837-1 (pdf e-book) --
ISBN 978-1-60882-838-8 (epub) 1. Interpersonal conflict. 2. Interpersonal relations. I. Title.
  BF637.I48M428 2013
  158.2--dc23                                    2013014287

Printed in the United States of America

24     23     22

10     9     8     7

*For my daughter, Bekah—*
*A beautiful, bright light.*
MM

*For my wife, Nancy Kesselring.*
PF

*For my parents, Agnes and Sam,*
*who've always been there for me.*
AL

*For Eric, Jake, and Kelly*
*For their love, support, and laughter.*
MS

# Contents

# Introduction

Interpersonal problems often occur across multiple relationships and areas of your life (friends, family, work, partner, and so on). These problems can trigger intense suffering for you and those you care for. If you are reading this book, you are likely struggling in some of your relationships, perhaps reacting in damaging ways to interpersonal stress. You may also have primary concerns such as anxiety, depression, or trauma coupled with relationship problems. You have probably found that treatments targeting your anxiety, depression, or trauma have not been very helpful in solving your interpersonal struggles.

We have combined ideas from schema-focused therapy with methods from acceptance and commitment therapy (ACT) to help you identify and change hurtful interpersonal patterns. This book focuses on ten schemas—abandonment/instability, mistrust/abuse, emotional deprivation, defectiveness/shame, social isolation/alienation, dependence, failure, entitlement/grandiosity, self-sacrifice/subjugation, and unrelenting standards/hypercriticalness—that are the deeply ingrained patterns of thought driving problematic coping behaviors. When situations or conversations trigger your schemas, your reaction is to protect yourself—avoid painful emotions. Unfortunately, your schema coping behaviors often make your relationships worse and increase your suffering.

This book provides you with an empirically-validated protocol—based on ACT—for addressing your interpersonal problems. You will learn to deal with schema-triggered pain differently, and to replace ineffective schema coping with responses based on your deepest values. Be warned: this is a "work" book—you must do the exercises in the book to make progress. At times, the process will be challenging and emotional, but it can result in greatly improved relationships. We all thrive when we are in loving, healthy relationships. Now, let's get started.

# CHAPTER 1

# Defining Interpersonal Problems

Do family gatherings leave you feeling isolated and alienated from your relatives? Can you name a long list of ex-friends you never hear from anymore? Have you had trouble maintaining a serious love relationship? Is your work life marked by friction with bosses and other employees? If the answers to these questions are predominantly yes, you may be suffering from interpersonal problems.

In this chapter you'll learn about the nature of interpersonal problems, what causes them, and how you can overcome them. The treatment program you'll be introduced to is research based (McKay, Lev, and Skeen 2012) and has been shown to be highly effective in changing problematic interpersonal behavior.

## What Are Interpersonal Problems?

*Interpersonal problems* are simply recurring relationship problems. If you have trouble relating to or getting along with family, friends, loved ones, colleagues, coworkers, and so on; the problems have been with you for a long time, come up frequently, and seem to follow a familiar pattern.

- *Example*

I'm June, a forty-eight-year-old real estate agent. I was fighting a lot with Ben, my third husband. He complained that I was too negative and not emotionally available to him. He seemed awfully needy to me, very grabby and clingy. I felt smothered around him. But I didn't want to get divorced. For one thing, I couldn't afford to pay for my rent and health insurance on my own. The real estate market was lousy from the day I got my license, and my commissions have never added up to a real living. I didn't hit it off with clients and did not develop the kind of repeat customers that other agents in my office had.

As for friends, I really only had one, an appraiser named Margie. We'd get together Friday nights to drink margaritas and make fun of everybody we knew in the local business community. Eventually life with Ben got so stressful that he and I agreed to separate for a while. Margie let me move into her guest room, and that was okay for about two weeks. We started to get on each other's nerves, and she eventually said it was time for me to move on.

●

# What Causes Interpersonal Problems?

Interpersonal problems are caused by *maladaptive coping strategies*: unhelpful ways in which you habitually deal with interpersonal stress. For example, when June's husband, Ben, accused her of being cold and distant, she coped with this interpersonal stress by attacking him: she accused him of smothering her and trying to micromanage their relationship.

*Attacking* is just one of the maladaptive coping strategies that can lead to an interpersonal problem. Some people who are faced with the same criticism might cope by *withdrawing*. They would escape the situation and the relationship by simply ignoring the criticism, refusing to talk about it, changing the subject, or leaving the room.

*Clinging* is another strategy that some people use to cope with interpersonal stress. They become very dependent on their loved ones, insisting that they cannot live without the relationship. It's a kind of emotional blackmail that says, "If you leave me, I'll collapse."

Another faulty coping mechanism is *blaming*. June might have blamed her husband for her distance from him, accusing him of pushing *her* away. Or she might have coped with the stress of his complaints by surrendering, saying immediately, "Oh, you're right. I'm sorry, I'll try harder," never really meaning to change, but just wanting the upset to end quickly.

Where do these faulty coping strategies come from? Many are learned in childhood, when they help people survive family life. For example, as a child, you might surrender to a domineering parent to stay safe. You might cope with a detached father by withdrawing or becoming clingy and overly compliant out of fear of abandonment. Sometimes children learn how to cope by copying what they see their parents doing: going on the attack when they feel frightened, or blaming others when they're hurt.

Some coping strategies are learned later on, when you stumble onto something that seems to help in social situations so you keep doing it. For example, Rick found out early in grade school that he could avoid some bullying and get some attention by cracking jokes and making his classmates laugh. He became the class clown, reacting to all kinds of social stress with humorous remarks. Unfortunately, he found later that he needed more than humor to succeed in marriage and a career.

That's the trouble with all these maladaptive coping mechanisms: in the short term, they help a little to protect you and cushion you from stress with certain people, so you keep using them. Over time they become inflexible, fixed patterns of behavior. You tend to react to all social situations the same way, time after time. The faulty coping strategies become generalized and pervasive: the way you handled your parents or your peers in third grade becomes the way you try to handle your adult friends, your lover, your spouse, or your boss. But what worked marginally back then works horribly now. The short-term strategy has become a long-term problem.

So you should just change coping strategies, right? That's not so easy, as June discovered.

## • *Example*

This is June again. I took a workshop from this super-salesman guy at the realty association. He told us very clearly how to behave when you're showing houses to prospective buyers: you should be positive at all times, pointing out the best features of the house. You should ask polite, personal questions and show interest in their kids and jobs. You should refrain from criticizing the seller or the house. Above all, you should answer all questions—however dumb—fully and clearly and patiently.

After the workshop, I was fired up, and I resolved to follow all the guidelines and start developing better rapport with my prospects. But people can be so stupid and irritating! They ask the same dumb questions over and over, and they don't pay attention to the answers. In about two weeks I was back to my old tricks: one-word answers, thinly veiled sarcasm, negativity, and impatience.

•

# What Makes Maladaptive Coping Strategies So Persistent?

If these ways of relating to others are so obviously unproductive, why is it so hard to change them? Because maladaptive coping strategies are not just simple habits reinforced by repetition; they arise from a deeper level, from almost-unconscious beliefs called *schemas*. Schemas are deeply held core beliefs about who you are as a person and the nature of your relationships to other people. Here are some typical schemas that can lead to interpersonal problems:

*People are always leaving me.*

*It's dangerous to trust people too much.*

*No one really cares for me or gives me what I need.*

*There's something wrong with me.*

*I don't belong anywhere.*

*I can't take care of myself; I need someone to help me.*

*Other people's needs are more important than mine. I have to put them first.*

*I should function at the highest level. Mistakes aren't acceptable.*

*Only the best is good enough for me.*

*I'm going to fail at what I do.*

If you have schemas like these, you act them out over time, developing those maladaptive coping strategies that are so hard to change. Your schemas guide not only your behavior, but also how you interpret other people's behavior. You see others in the light of your schemas, noticing their negative words and actions that reinforce your schemas and filtering out anything that contradicts your core beliefs.

Your schemas are deeply ingrained, and they persist because they help you understand the world and organize your life. A schema like *It's dangerous to trust people too much* can serve as a guideline in many situations, making you feel safe and independent and strong—at least in the short term, until loneliness and isolation lead to chronic depression and resentment.

- *Example*

I'm Ross. I'm twenty-nine years old. I've always felt that I'm damaged goods, that no one could really love me if they knew the real me. That's the schema that runs my love life. Whenever I start getting close to someone, I'm afraid she'll see how messed up I am. So I tend to dump women before they can dump me. It's a way of protecting myself, rejecting someone before she can reject me.

   I tried to change with my last girlfriend, Irene. I resolved to hang in there when she started talking about how well we got along and hinting about moving in together. But the pressure built up, and I got more and more tense around Irene until, finally, one night I started a big argument and we broke up. It was weird—I could almost watch myself doing exactly what I had planned not to do, but I couldn't stop doing it. At this point, I'm not open to any new relationships. They're too painful and bound to fail.

   •

# How Can You Overcome Interpersonal Problems?

To overcome interpersonal problems, you need to set and accomplish four essential goals. First, you have to change problem behaviors, such as habitually bragging or harshly criticizing or angrily lashing out at people. Second, to get along with different kinds of people, you need to develop some behavioral flexibility: a range of social responses that are appropriate to a range of situations. Third, you need to detach yourself from some negative, self-defeating beliefs about yourself and others. Fourth and finally, you have to learn how to stop avoiding the social situations in which you feel uncomfortable.

   To accomplish these four essential goals, this book combines techniques from acceptance and commitment therapy (ACT) developed by Steven Hayes and associates (Hayes, Strosahl, and Wilson 1999) and schema therapy developed by Jeffrey Young and associates (Young, Klosko, and Weishaar 2006). As you work through this book, you will learn to deal with your interpersonal problems by taking these six steps:

1. Uncover your schemas.

2. Identify your maladaptive coping strategies.

3. Identify your core values about how you want to be in your relationships.

4. Learn to observe and accept schema pain without acting on it.

5. Learn to distance yourself from painful schema-driven thoughts.

6. Turn values—who you want to be in your relationships—into action.

This approach has been proven to work by Avigail Lev, who, in 2011, conducted a randomized controlled trial of these techniques that showed significant decreases in problematic interpersonal behaviors (Lev 2011; McKay, Lev, and Skeen 2012).

# CHAPTER 2

# Identifying Schemas

In this chapter you will identify the maladaptive schemas that underlie your interpersonal problems. A *maladaptive schema* (Young 1999) is essentially a belief about yourself and your relationship to the world—the core sense and feeling is that something is wrong with you, with your relationships, or with the world at large. These schemas interfere with your ability to feel safe and to satisfy your basic needs in relationships to others. Jeffrey Young and associates (Young, Klosko, and Weishaar 2006) developed a treatment—Schema Therapy—that identified the particular schemas you'll explore below.

## How Schemas Are Formed and Take Hold

Maladaptive schemas are formed in childhood and develop as a result of ongoing, dysfunctional experiences with parents, siblings, and peers. They come from specific traumatic events or from repeated toxic messages that you receive about yourself: "You're bad" or "You don't do anything right." Maladaptive schemas are reinforced as you grow up and as you try to make sense of your experience and avoid further pain.

Once a schema is formed, it's extremely stable and becomes an enduring pattern that is elaborated throughout your life. A schema is like a pair of sunglasses that color your reality, changing the way you see things and leading you to make assumptions and predictions about every situation you encounter.

The schemas formed in childhood get triggered over and over again in adult life by stressful interpersonal events. When a schema is triggered, it brings up specific, automatic, powerful thoughts and feelings. These can lead to chronic emotional problems with depression, panic, loneliness, or anger. These thoughts and feelings can also result in interpersonal problems in which, because of the schema, you respond to others in ways that hurt your relationships.

# Uncovering Your Schemas

You can identify your early maladaptive schemas by the following characteristics:

- Unconditional. You experience them as obvious truths about yourself or your environment.

- Resistant to change. They are an ingrained pattern since childhood.

- Self-perpetuating. They trigger behavior that seems to confirm the truth of the schema.

- Predictive. They help you predict what will happen in future relationships, and because they create the illusion that you can see what's coming, they are extremely difficult to give up.

- Triggered by social stress. They are activated when something painful happens in a relationship.

- Highly emotional. They always are accompanied by strong feelings of shame, fear, hurt, despair, and so on.

---

## Exercise 2.1 Identify Your Schemas

After reading each of the one hundred statements that follow (adapted from McKay and Fanning 1991), circle "T" or "F" according to whether you think the statement is mostly true or mostly false. In cases where it's a close decision, go with your first impulse. It's important to complete every item, circling the "T" or the "F" (but not both), in order to get an accurate score at the end. But this is not a test; there are no right or wrong answers.

| Mostly True | Mostly False | Statement | |
|:---:|:---:|:---|:---|
| T | F | 1. | *Most of my loved ones are stable and dependable.* |
| T | F | 2. | *I seldom feel taken advantage of.* |
| T | F | 3. | *I feel loved and cared for.* |
| T | F | 4. | *I am worthy of love and respect.* |
| T | F | 5. | *I feel a strong sense of belonging in my family and community.* |
| T | F | 6. | *In most situations, I manage to do what needs to be done.* |

T     F     7.   *I perform many tasks well.*

T     F     8.   *I feel pretty average most of the time.*

T     F     9.   *I can rely on myself to get what I need.*

T     F     10.   *I set reasonable standards for myself.*

T     F     11.   *Significant people in my life are unstable.*

T     F     12.   *Many people would like to hurt me or take advantage of me.*

T     F     13.   *I've never really felt cared for by my family.*

T     F     14.   *I often feel flawed or defective.*

T     F     15.   *I frequently feel left out of groups.*

T     F     16.   *I feel incompetent in many situations.*

T     F     17.   *I'm basically a screwup.*

T     F     18.   *I'm a superior type of person.*

T     F     19.   *Others can care for me better than I can care for myself.*

T     F     20.   *Very little of what I do satisfies me; I usually think I could do better.*

T     F     21.   *I feel secure and safe.*

T     F     22.   *I tend to trust people and give them the benefit of the doubt.*

T     F     23.   *I have at least one satisfying intimate relationship.*

T     F     24.   *I feel okay about myself.*

T     F     25.   *I fit in well with my circle of friends.*

T     F     26.   *I can survive on my own for long periods of time.*

T     F     27.   *Doing some things comes easily for me.*

T     F     28.   *I'm only human; I make my share of mistakes.*

T     F     29.   *It's okay to disagree with others.*

T     F     30.   *I can forgive myself for failure.*

T     F     31.   *I've never really felt protected and safeguarded in my family.*

T     F     32.   *Most people cannot be trusted.*

T     F     33.   *My relationships are shallow; if I disappeared tomorrow, no one would notice.*

T     F     34.   *Nobody I desire would desire me if they really got to know me.*

T     F     35.   *I feel like an outsider.*

| | | | |
|---|---|---|---|
| T | F | 36. | *I feel that certain people are essential for my survival.* |
| T | F | 37. | *When I trust my own judgment, I make wrong decisions.* |
| T | F | 38. | *I have many more excellent qualities than the average person.* |
| T | F | 39. | *I find myself going along with others' plans.* |
| T | F | 40. | *I'm a perfectionist; I must be the best at whatever I do.* |
| T | F | 41. | *I can count on at least one person in my life to always be there for me.* |
| T | F | 42. | *I rarely need to protect or guard myself with other people.* |
| T | F | 43. | *I feel nurtured in my family.* |
| T | F | 44. | *I have legitimate needs I deserve to fill.* |
| T | F | 45. | *People usually accept me as I am.* |
| T | F | 46. | *I rarely need or ask for help from others.* |
| T | F | 47. | *I am a skillful person, as capable as most people.* |
| T | F | 48. | *I am content with my fair share and don't need any special consideration.* |
| T | F | 49. | *I don't need the approval of others for everything I do.* |
| T | F | 50. | *I set achievable goals for myself.* |
| T | F | 51. | *People are always leaving me.* |
| T | F | 52. | *I must be on my guard against other people's lies and hostile remarks.* |
| T | F | 53. | *Most of my family members are cold and distant.* |
| T | F | 54. | *I'm dull and boring and can't make interesting conversation.* |
| T | F | 55. | *People don't usually include me in what they're doing.* |
| T | F | 56. | *I depend heavily on others for help.* |
| T | F | 57. | *I tend to avoid new challenges.* |
| T | F | 58. | *I feel I deserve some special privileges or consideration.* |
| T | F | 59. | *I don't function well on my own.* |
| T | F | 60. | *Failure is very upsetting to me.* |
| T | F | 61. | *I have people I can really rely on.* |
| T | F | 62. | *You can count on most people to do what they say they will do.* |
| T | F | 63. | *I can get the care and attention I need.* |
| T | F | 64. | *I count for something in the world.* |

| | | | |
|---|---|---|---|
| T | F | 65. | *My hopes and dreams are much like everyone else's.* |
| T | F | 66. | *I am confident that I can handle most problems.* |
| T | F | 67. | *I can learn new skills if I try.* |
| T | F | 68. | *I deserve the same treatment as anyone else, no more, no less.* |
| T | F | 69. | *I like to spend time by myself.* |
| T | F | 70. | *I'm not perfect, and that's okay.* |
| T | F | 71. | *Some people who are important to me are unreliable.* |
| T | F | 72. | *Many people will break their promises and lie.* |
| T | F | 73. | *There's no one I can count on for care and advice.* |
| T | F | 74. | *I'm unattractive.* |
| T | F | 75. | *Sometimes I feel like an alien, very different from everybody else.* |
| T | F | 76. | *I often feel helpless or at a loss concerning what to do.* |
| T | F | 77. | *I don't perform well under stress.* |
| T | F | 78. | *I feel that I shouldn't have to accept some of the limitations placed on ordinary people.* |
| T | F | 79. | *I try hard to please others, and I put their needs before my own.* |
| T | F | 80. | *I push myself so hard that I harm my relationships, my health, or my happiness.* |
| T | F | 81. | *I have at least one solid, stable relationship.* |
| T | F | 82. | *I feel confident that I will be treated well by others.* |
| T | F | 83. | *I can depend on my friends for advice and emotional support.* |
| T | F | 84. | *People I like and respect often like and respect me.* |
| T | F | 85. | *I could change jobs or join a club and soon fit in.* |
| T | F | 86. | *I don't need to ask for assistance very often.* |
| T | F | 87. | *Most of my decisions are sound.* |
| T | F | 88. | *When it comes to the good things in life, I mostly get what I deserve.* |
| T | F | 89. | *I think for myself; I can stand up for my ideas.* |
| T | F | 90. | *It's okay to make mistakes.* |
| T | F | 91. | *I'm afraid of being abandoned, that a loved one will die or reject me.* |
| T | F | 92. | *So many people have let me down.* |

| | | | |
|---|---|---|---|
| T | F | 93. | *I have no one who hugs me, shares secrets with me, or really cares what happens to me.* |
| T | F | 94. | *I don't deserve much attention or respect.* |
| T | F | 95. | *I don't feel that I belong where I am.* |
| T | F | 96. | *I frequently need assistance from others.* |
| T | F | 97. | *I mess up everything I attempt.* |
| T | F | 98. | *I'm entitled to the best that life has to offer.* |
| T | F | 99. | *I have trouble making my own wants and needs known.* |
| T | F | 100. | *I have very clear, black-and-white rules for myself.* |

## Scoring

This inventory assesses your core beliefs about the ten topics that follow. These topics are important areas of everyone's life, about which everyone has some sort of belief, whether it is conscious or not.

To score your answers, follow these instructions carefully:

1.  Abandonment/Instability:              ____

    Look at your answers for items 1, 21, 41, 61, and 81. For each "F" circled, give yourself one point.

    Now look at your answers for items 11, 31, 51, 71, and 91. For each "T" circled, give yourself one point. Record your total points above.

    On a scale from 0 to 10, this indicates how much you agree with the statement, *Significant people in my life are unstable or unreliable.*

2.  Mistrust/Abuse:              ____

    Look at your answers for items 2, 22, 42, 62, and 82. For each "F" circled, give yourself one point.

    Now look at your answers for items 12, 32, 52, 72, and 92. For each "T" circled, give yourself one point. Record your total points above.

    On a scale from 0 to 10, this indicates how much you agree with the statement, *I'll be hurt by abuse or neglect.*

3.   Emotional Deprivation: _____

Look at your answers for items 3, 23, 43, 63, and 83. For each "F" circled, give yourself one point.

Now look at your answers for items 13, 33, 53, 73, and 93. For each "T" circled, give yourself one point. Record your total points above.

On a scale from 0 to 10, this indicates how much you agree with the statement, *My need for emotional support will not be met.*

4.   Defectiveness/Shame: _____

Look at your answers for items 4, 24, 44, 64, and 84. For each "F" circled, give yourself one point.

Now look at your answers for items 14, 34, 54, 74, and 94. For each "T" circled, give yourself one point. Record your total points above.

On a scale from 0 to 10, this indicates how much you agree with the statement, *I'm defective, inferior, unlovable.*

5.   Social Isolation/Alienation: _____

Look at your answers for items 5, 25, 45, 65, and 85. For each "F" circled, give yourself one point.

Now look at your answers for items 15, 35, 55, 75, and 95. For each "T" circled, give yourself one point. Record your total points above.

On a scale from 0 to 10, this indicates how much you agree with the statement, *I do not belong to a group; I'm isolated or different from others.*

6.   Dependence: _____

Look at your answers for items 6, 26, 46, 66, and 86. For each "F" circled, give yourself one point.

Now look at your answers for items 16, 36, 56, 76, and 96. For each "T" circled, give yourself one point. Record your total points above.

On a scale from 0 to 10, this indicates how much you agree with the statement, *I am incompetent or helpless; I need significant assistance from others and/or I can't survive without another.*

7. Failure: ____

Look at your answers for items 7, 27, 47, 67, and 87. For each "F" circled, give yourself one point.

Now look at your answers for items 17, 37, 57, 77, and 97. For each "T" circled, give yourself one point. Record your total points above.

On a scale from 0 to 10, this indicates how much you agree with the statement, *I am inadequate and will ultimately fail.*

8. Entitlement/Grandiosity: ____

Look at your answers for items 8, 28, 48, 68, and 88. For each "F" circled, give yourself one point.

Now look at your answers for items 18, 38, 58, 78, and 98. For each "T" circled, give yourself one point. Record your total points above.

On a scale from 0 to 10, this indicates how much you agree with the statement, *I'm superior to others; I deserve special privileges.*

9. Self-Sacrifice/Subjugation: ____

Look at your answers for items 9, 29, 49, 69, and 89. For each "F" circled, give yourself one point.

Now look at your answers for items 19, 39, 59, 79, and 99. For each "T" circled, give yourself one point. Record your total points above.

On a scale from 0 to 10, this indicates how much you agree with the statement, *I meet others' needs before mine, either voluntarily or through real or perceived coercion.*

10. Unrelenting Standards/Hypercriticalness: ____

Look at your answers for items 10, 30, 50, 70, and 90. For each "F" circled, give yourself one point.

Now look at your answers for items 20, 40, 60, 80, and 100. For each "T" circled, give yourself one point. Record your total points above.

On a scale from 0 to 10, this indicates how much you agree with the statement, *I must meet my very high standards to avoid criticism by others.*

How did you do? One way to visualize these results is to enter your scores on the following bar chart. For each of the ten schemas, color in the bar up to the height of your score.

Scale (10 down to 1) for each of the following columns:

1. Abandonment/Instability
2. Mistrust/Abuse
3. Emotional Deprivation
4. Defectiveness/Shame
5. Social Isolation/Alienation
6. Dependence
7. Failure
8. Entitlement/Grandiosity
9. Self-Sacrifice/Subjugation
10. Unrelenting Standards/Hypercriticalness

You might think of these bars as the bars of the "Interpersonal Problems Prison." If most of the bars are low, you can escape the prison more easily. If most of the bars are high, it will take more time and effort to get out of schema jail.

On the other hand, don't think of these ten items as cast in iron, as the only possible schemas involved in interpersonal problems. Ten is just a convenient number, and the exact wording of each schema is a kind of average of what many people have reported believing. You're an individual, and the number and phrasing of your schemas will be unique to you.

# Exercise 2.2 Thought Log

A way to uncover your unique schemas is to start with something more obvious: your feelings and thoughts in real-life social situations. Use the following log for two weeks. During that period, pay attention to all of your social interactions, and notice any painful emotions that come up: anxiety, embarrassment, anger, sadness, and so on. Whenever you feel an unpleasant emotion, write down the situation and the feeling as soon as you can, followed by a brief description of the thoughts you were thinking at the time.

# Thought Log

| Situation | Feelings | Thoughts |
|-----------|----------|----------|
|           |          |          |
|           |          |          |
|           |          |          |
|           |          |          |
|           |          |          |
|           |          |          |
|           |          |          |
|           |          |          |
|           |          |          |

- *Example*

Hi, I'm Jason. I'm thirty-six years old. Here are three items from the Thought Log that I kept for two weeks. I found that my worst feelings came up when I was dealing with my wife, my daughter, and my boss at work.

# Thought Log

| Situation | Feelings | Thoughts |
|---|---|---|
| *Performance review with boss; she says I need to be more of a team player.* | *Anxious* | *She's building a case to fire me. I'm such a screwup. I'll never get another job this good.* |
| *Helping daughter with algebra homework; she just doesn't get it.* | *Depressed, angry* | *I can't stand this!* |
| *Wife calls from her mother's house, says she's decided to stay overnight and come home tomorrow.* | *Scared* | *She's planning to leave me.* |

- 

# Exercise 2.3 Drilling Down through Thoughts to Schemas

It's unlikely that the thoughts you record in your Thought Log will be clear, succinct statements of your schemas. These thoughts are probably familiar parts of your day-to-day internal monologue, a mixture of observations, interpretations, memories, and predictions that are only loosely based on your schemas.

To drill down through your surface thoughts to the schemas beneath, ask yourself this question:

*If* _____ (the thought) *is true, what does that mean about me?*

The answer is a second thought that will be closer to a schema. Use it to ask the question again:

*If* _____ (the second thought) *is true, what does that mean about me?*

Keep asking yourself the same question about each new thought until you end up with a statement that feels like a rock-bottom fact about yourself. That is likely to be one of your schemas.

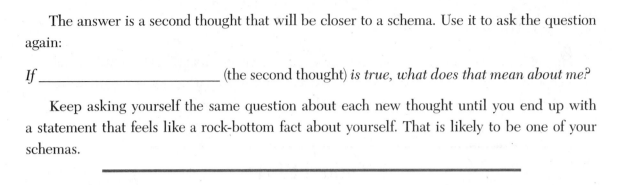

## •  *Example*

This is Jason again. I did the drilling-down exercise with the thought I had while I was trying to help my daughter with her math homework. The original thought was *I can't stand this!*

I asked myself, *If it's true that I can't stand this, what does that mean about me?*

I answered, *It means that I can't deal with her resistance, the way she just ignores what I want her to do.*

So I asked myself, *If it's true that she resists me and ignores what I want her to do, what does that mean about me?*

The answer was, *It means I'm a screwed-up parent. I don't know what I'm doing.*

Then I asked myself, *If it's true that I don't know what I'm doing as a parent, what does that mean about me?*

The answer to that one was *It means I'm a failure. I don't have any parenting skills.*

At that point, I realized I had hit bottom, with a very basic, very sad thought about myself. I also noticed that it was very close to some of the statements from the "Failure" part of the schema inventory.

•

# Exercise 2.4 Schema Imagery

Another way to clarify your schemas is through imagery. You visualize a stressful social interaction, reliving it in your imagination, and slow it down and analyze it so that you can observe your feelings and thoughts.

*Find a quiet place where you won't be disturbed for ten minutes. Lie or sit with your legs and arms uncrossed. Close your eyes and take several slow, deep breaths. Think back to a recent, typical social situation in which you experienced negative emotions.*

*Take your time and really re-create the scene in your mind's eye. Notice the setting: the colors and shapes, sounds and smells, textures and tones. Make the scene as real as you can in your mind's eye. See the other person or people, and be yourself in the scene. Run it like a movie from start to finish, saying what you said, hearing what you heard, doing what you did. Watch and hear the other person acting out his or her part.*

*What are you afraid will happen in this scene?*

*How does the other person see you in this scene?*

*What does this scene make you feel about yourself? Let yourself feel the same feelings that you had at the time: shyness, embarrassment, nervousness, fear, irritation, anger, shame, guilt. Give the feeling a name and say it out loud.*

*What are you telling yourself during this scene? Put it into words and say it out loud.*

The answers to these questions will often provide a clear description of your schemas.

---

## • *Example*

Hi, I'm Clare. I'm twenty-eight years old. I used schema imagery to analyze a scene I had with my husband, Clark. I visualized Clark coming home from work and coming down to the basement where I was doing laundry. I imagined hearing the buzzing fluorescent lights and smelling the damp basement smell.

Clark sees that the laundry sink is still leaking into the bucket that's been under it for two weeks. He says, "Didn't you call the plumber?"

I immediately feel guilty and panicky, and my eyes tear up. I don't say anything; I just look down into the washing machine.

"Well?" he says.

"But you always call the plumber," I say.

"I've been working overtime for fourteen days straight," he says. "You've got to help take up the slack."

"I tried," I say, starting to cry.

He sighs, shaking his head and saying nothing more.

And then I just weep, feeling depressed and useless.

It's not a violent scene or a dramatic one, but it's so typical.

What I'm afraid of in this scene is that Clark will finally get fed up with me. I think that he hates how dependent I am on him, how I hang on him like a dead weight. This scene makes me feel incompetent, incomplete, and helpless to do anything for myself. The one word for this schema is "dependent."

●

# Schemas and Painful Emotions

Now that you have uncovered your schemas about relationships, you can explore the painful emotions that result. Each schema is typically associated with one or more painful emotional states. Because schema beliefs and schema emotions always go hand in hand, you have learned to fear those moments of interpersonal stress when schemas get triggered. The following table identifies the typical emotions for each of the ten schemas.

| Schema | Emotions |
| --- | --- |
| Abandonment/Instability | Fear, anger, and grief |
| Mistrust/Abuse | Fear and anger |
| Emotional Deprivation | Loneliness, yearning, sadness, and anger |
| Defectiveness/Shame | Shame, sadness, and anger |
| Social Isolation/Alienation | Loneliness, shame, fear, anxiety, anger, and yearning |
| Dependence | Fear, anxiety, and anger |
| Failure | Fear, sadness, anger, and shame |
| Entitlement/Grandiosity | Anger |
| Self-Sacrifice/Subjugation | Guilt and fear |
| Unrelenting Standards/Hypercriticalness | Anger |

## Exercise 2.5 Identify Schema-Based Emotions

Use the following chart to identify the particular painful emotions that come up when your schemas get triggered. In the first column, list the schemas you have uncovered in this chapter. Then visualize the kind of situations in which each schema is triggered, and in the second column, list the emotions you experience.

| Schema | Emotions |
|--------|----------|
|        |          |
|        |          |
|        |          |
|        |          |
|        |          |
|        |          |
|        |          |

# Avoidance

As humans, we all want to get away from pain. We fear painful emotions, and often we seek relief when they show up. When painful schema feelings get triggered, we often feel desperate to get away from them. This results in the maladaptive coping strategies discussed in chapter 1: the schema coping behaviors that get us into trouble in relationships.

Here is the sequence: a stressful interpersonal situation triggers a schema thought, which in turn brings up a painful emotion, which creates an urge to get away, which triggers a habitual avoidance strategy.

EVENT  →  SCHEMA  →  EMOTION  →  URGE  →  AVOIDANCE

## •  *Example*

Hi, I'm Roger. I'm forty-two years old, and I manage a motel in a small resort town. I dropped in at the department of motor vehicles to get the answer to a very simple question about replacing a lost license plate. They wanted me to take a number and wait, instead of taking ten seconds to just answer my simple question. This triggered my schema about being entitled to better treatment than that, which triggered a flash of anger. I felt so pissed off that I just had to get away, so I turned on my heel and stormed out of there, without the answer to my question.

•

In the sequence EVENT  →  SCHEMA  →  EMOTION  →  URGE  →  AVOIDANCE, it is not the emotion or the urge to get away that is the problem. The problem is the avoidance: acting on your urge to escape the painful feelings. Avoidance of schema pain *creates* interpersonal problems. The next two chapters will explain in detail exactly how this works.

# CHAPTER 3

# Schema Triggers

A schema is like a lens that changes and distorts what you see. Once your schemas are triggered, you end up viewing yourself and your relationships in ways that plunge you into a great deal of emotional pain. You can't avoid schema triggers. But learning to recognize your triggers will help you make better choices for how you respond.

## Recognizing Schema Triggers

Let's look at each of the ten maladaptive schemas that affect relationships, the typical situations that can trigger them, and the negative feelings that result (adapted from *Acceptance and Commitment Therapy for Interpersonal Problems* [McKay, Lev, and Skeen 2012]).

- *Abandonment/Instability:* An abandonment schema will likely get triggered when you are with someone who is unpredictable, unstable, or unavailable. When this schema gets triggered, feelings of anger, fear, and grief will surface.

- *Mistrust/Abuse:* A mistrust/abuse schema will likely get triggered when you are interacting with anyone who you perceive will hurt or betray you. When this schema is triggered, you will experience feelings of anger and fear.

- *Emotional Deprivation:* An emotional deprivation schema will likely get triggered if you feel lonely, if you are with a detached partner, or if you don't feel understood, protected, or loved. The feelings that will surface when this schema is triggered are sadness, anger, and depression (often experienced as loneliness or yearning).

- *Defectiveness/Shame:* A defectiveness/shame schema will likely get triggered when you start to get close to someone and fear that your defects will be exposed, when you are criticized by others, or when you are in a situation that makes you fear that others will find you inadequate, flawed, or unworthy. The primary emotions that surface when this schema is triggered are shame, anger, and sadness.

- *Social Isolation/Alienation:* A social isolation/alienation schema will get triggered when you are in situations or with groups of people that make you feel different or left out. Emotions that dominate when this schema is triggered are fear, anxiety, anger, shame, and loneliness.

- *Dependence:* A dependence schema will likely get triggered by any life changes, any new situations, or the ending of a relationship with the person you rely on the most. Anxiety, fear, and anger are the predominant emotions when this schema is triggered.

- *Failure:* A failure schema will likely get triggered when you are with other people who are more successful, or in situations that make you feel that you lack in the areas of accomplishments, special talents, competence, or intelligence. The primary emotions that surface are depression, shame, fear, and anger.

- *Entitlement/Grandiosity:* An entitlement/grandiosity schema will likely get triggered when things don't go your way or when your needs and desires are not put first. The primary emotion that surfaces when this schema gets triggered is anger.

- *Self-sacrifice/Subjugation:* A self-sacrifice/subjugation schema will get triggered when you are in situations and relationships where the needs of others come first or you feel controlled by others. You feel trapped in life and in relationships. The primary emotions associated with the triggering of this schema are fear and guilt.

- *Unrelenting Standards/Hypercriticalness:* An unrelenting standards/hypercriticalness schema will get triggered when you feel that you or others have not met your high standards. The primary emotion associated with the triggering of this schema is anger.

- *Example*

My name is Beth, and I'm twenty-eight years old. The schemas that affect me most are failure and abandonment/instability. Both of them have a big impact on my relationships, particularly with my boyfriend and my father. When I read through the typical triggers for each schema, I saw the types of situations that set off my feelings of failure or fear of abandonment.

My boyfriend is busy all the time, and my father is a writer who's totally incommunicado when he's in the middle of a project. That's what presses my abandonment button—when I can't reach them or they're putting me off.

And with failure, I get triggered by criticism. My father is always talking about the things that I mess up, how I'm not careful enough. And my boyfriend triggers me when he keeps pushing me to go back to school—as if I'm a failure because I didn't finish and now work as only a secretary.

- 

## Exercise 3.1 Schema Triggers Worksheet

Not only does each schema have its own typical triggers, but also these triggers can show up in every relationship domain (work, friends, family, intimate relationships, parenting, and community). This exercise will help you recognize how schemas get triggered and which schemas show up at work and with various friends, family, and so on. For every domain, think about specific people and the conflicts and issues that upset you. Fill in the schemas and the schema-driven emotions that show up with these people. Then identify the specific triggering situations and the accompanying feelings. Go ahead and fill in the worksheet, trying to remember each relationship that triggers you and collecting as much information as possible about your schemas in each domain.

# Schema Triggers Worksheet

| Domain | Schema | Trigger Situations | Emotions |
|--------|--------|--------------------|----------|
|        |        |                    |          |
|        |        |                    |          |
|        |        |                    |          |
|        |        |                    |          |
|        |        |                    |          |

- *Example*

My name is Joaquin. I am twenty-nine years old. I've been struggling with three schemas. Recognizing them has been upsetting, yet I'm starting to understand things that I didn't get before—like why they happened. My schemas are defectiveness/shame, social isolation/alienation, and self-sacrifice/subjugation. You can see the situations that trigger them in my worksheet.

## Joaquin's Schema Triggers Worksheet

| Domain | Schema | Trigger Situations | Emotions |
|---|---|---|---|
| Work | Social Isolation/ Alienation | Everybody goes to lunch in little cliques. | anger, sadness |
| | Social Isolation/ Alienation | Not included in marketing task force. | anger |
| | Defectiveness/Shame | Any criticism/negative feedback. | shame, anger |
| Friends | Self-Sacrifice/ Subjugation | Any time there's a conflict between what they want and what I want. | anxiety, resentment |
| | Social Isolation/ Alienation | When I find out that friends did something together without including me. | anger, sadness |
| | Defectiveness/Shame | When I'm teased or criticized. | |
| | Defectiveness/Shame | When I call and they don't call back. | shame, anger sadness, anger |
| Family | Defectiveness/Shame | My mother complains that I'm not married. | anger |
| | Social Isolation/ Alienation | When my family gathers, they seem comfortable talking to each other, but not to me. | hurt, anger |
| | Self-Sacrifice/ Subjugation | When my mother asks me to do things I don't want to do. | anxiety, resentment |
| Intimate Relationships | Self-Sacrifice/ Subjugation | I always feel I have to do what the other person wants on dates. | anxiety, resentment |
| | Defectiveness/Shame | Any criticism on a date about anything I do. | shame, anger |
| Community | Social Isolation/ Alienation | No one really talks to me at my activism meetings. | anger, sadness |
| | Defectiveness/Shame | People who get angry when I try to register them to vote. | anger, shame |

•

Notice that Joaquin's worksheet records multiple schemas in most relationship domains. This is typical. The same schemas are often triggered in many different relationships. Conversely, the same relationship can trigger several very different schemas.

It's also worth noticing that each schema has only a few characteristic triggers. With Joaquin, for example, the defectiveness/shame schema is usually triggered by criticism or another person's anger. The social isolation/alienation schema is typically triggered when Joaquin is ignored by a group.

---

# Exercise 3.2 Schema Events Record

It's important to start applying what you've just learned to experiences in your relationships right now. To do that, you need to observe the triggers *when they happen*. Any time you notice sudden negative emotions in a relationship, it means your schemas have just been triggered. The point right now is not to control the schemas and painful emotions, but to recognize the *moment* when the schema and the schema emotions get activated.

The following Schema Events Record will help you track schema triggers as they occur. Each time a negative feeling comes up in one of your relationships, note in the Schema Events Record what triggered it, and name the schema and the accompanying emotion. We recommend keeping the Schema Events Record right by your bed and making these notes each night. Learning to mindfully watch each schema-triggering event prepares you to make new responses, new choices. But you're not ready for that yet; for now, you are just watching.

# Schema Events Record

| Schema-Triggering Event | Schema | Emotions |
|---|---|---|
|  |  |  |

Now that you know what situations precipitate schemas and schema emotions, you can be alert and watch for them in everyday life. In the next chapter, you'll use this knowledge to begin tracking how you react to schemas and how they affect your relationships.

# CHAPTER 4

# How Schemas Affect Your Relationships

*Schema coping behaviors* (SCBs), identified by Young and associates (Young, Klosko, and Weishaar 2006), are strategies that help you manage or block schema pain. Those schema feelings—fear, shame, anger, and despair—are so powerful that you immediately try to suppress them. SCBs give you temporary relief, but in the long run, they not only make schema pain worse, but also often destroy relationships.

Schema coping behaviors are frequently learned from watching your own family. Your father may have gone on the attack when he was hurt. Your mother may have withdrawn when she felt helpless. SCBs take many forms but share a common element: they seek to keep schema pain at bay.

## How Schema Coping Behaviors Hurt You

Early in life, when a maladaptive schema got triggered, you learned a response that controlled the pain. And you've used it again and again in similar situations. The trouble with schema coping behaviors is that they tend to hurt others. When you withdraw, collapse, or go into attack mode, the relationship suffers. After a while, people get tired of the unpleasant ways in which you cope with schema pain. They harden or withdraw, and you may lose them.

There are ten schema coping behaviors, divided into three main categories: The first is attack/overcompensation, where you become aggressive in response to a schema-triggering event. The second is surrender, where you are passive and acquiescing in the face of schema triggers. The last is avoidance, where you attempt to completely get away from the triggering situation.

| Category | Schema Coping Behaviors |
|---|---|
| Attack/ Overcompensation | 1. *Aggression, Hostility:* If you use this coping behavior in response to a schema-triggering event, you will find yourself counterattacking by blaming, criticizing, challenging, or being resistant. <br> 2. *Dominance, Excessive Self-Assertion:* If you use this coping behavior, you will find yourself taking control of others in order to accomplish your goals. <br> 3. *Recognition Seeking, Status Seeking:* If you use this coping behavior, you will find yourself overcompensating by trying to impress others and getting attention through high achievement and status. <br> 4. *Manipulation, Exploitation:* If you use this coping behavior, you will find yourself trying to meet your own needs without letting others know what you are doing. It may involve the use of seduction or not being completely truthful to others. <br> 5. *Passive-Aggressiveness, Rebellion:* If you use this coping behavior, you will appear to be compliant, but actually will be rebelling by procrastinating, complaining, being tardy, or not performing. |
| Surrender | 6. *Compliance, Dependence:* If you use this coping behavior in response to a schema-triggering event, you will find yourself relying on others, giving in, being dependent, behaving passively, avoiding conflict, and pleasing others. |
| Avoidance | 7. *Social Withdrawal, Excessive Autonomy:* If you use this coping behavior, you will find yourself isolating socially, disconnecting, and withdrawing from others. You may appear to be excessively independent and self-reliant because of your lack of involvement with others. You may engage in more solitary activities, such as reading, TV watching, computer use, or solitary work. <br> 8. *Compulsive Stimulation Seeking:* If you use this coping behavior in response to a schema-triggering event, you will find yourself seeking excitement or distraction through shopping, sex, risk taking, or physical activity. <br> 9. *Addictive Self-Soothing:* If you use this coping behavior, you will find yourself seeking excitement with drugs, alcohol, food, or excessive self-stimulation. <br> 10. *Psychological Withdrawal:* If you use this coping behavior, you will find yourself escaping through dissociation, denial, fantasy, or other internal forms of withdrawal. |

# Exercise 4.1 Schema Coping Behaviors Worksheet

Now that you know what schema coping behaviors look like, it's time to link them to your triggers. It's important to see how you cope in each situation that activates a schema. To begin this process, go back to the Schema Triggers Worksheet you filled out in the last chapter. Look at the "Trigger Situations" column, and transfer these items to the "Schema-Triggering Situations" on the SCB Worksheet that follows. Now, in the "Schema Coping Behaviors" column, describe the SCB you used for each trigger.

If you have difficulty remembering exactly what you did, try visualizing a particular triggering situation. Then:

1. Let yourself feel the emotion.

2. Notice what the emotion pushes you to do. How do you want to cope with this pain?

3. Look back at the list of ten schema coping behaviors.

4. Identify which SCBs you used.

# Schema Coping Behaviors Worksheet

| Schema-Triggering Situations | Schema Coping Behaviors |
| --- | --- |
|  |  |

Which schema coping behaviors do you rely on most often? And which situations typically set off a particular SCB? Armed with this knowledge, you can (1) start to recognize triggers *as they occur* in real time and (2) notice your coping response. Eventually, changing your behavior depends on seeing both the trigger and the impulse to cope *in the moment*. This is hard. It can make you feel ashamed or like a failure as you notice SCBs in daily life. *There I go again* is sometimes the feeling. Be gentle with yourself as you notice the ways in which you cope with schema pain. Awareness comes first. Then comes change.

## • *Example*

Hi, this is Joaquin again. Here's how I filled out my SCB Worksheet.

# Joaquin's SCB Worksheet

| Schema-Triggering Situations | Schema Coping Behaviors |
| --- | --- |
| *Everybody goes to lunch in little cliques.* | Withdraw, *refuse to talk to anybody.* |
| *Not included in marketing task force.* | Withdraw, *refuse to help on another project.* |
| *Criticism/negative feedback.* | Attack, *tell them it's bullshit.* |
| *Conflict between my needs and theirs.* | Surrender, *give in, get a little sullen.* |
| *Friends doing something that doesn't include me.* | Withdraw, *stop calling people. Complain about them to others* (passive-aggressive). |
| *Teased.* | Attack, *find something wrong with the person.* |
| *Someone doesn't return my call.* | Complain *to others, act cold or shut down if I see the person.* |
| *Mother complains that I'm not married.* | Attack ("*I can't find anybody who isn't like you.*") |
| *Everyone in the family is talking except me.* | Withdraw, *refuse to talk.* |
| *Mother asks me to do things I don't want to do.* | Surrender, *give in, get sullen.* |
| *Criticized by someone I'm dating.* | Withdraw, *stop talking.* |
| *Pressure to do what the other person wants on dates.* | Surrender, *go along, try to be nice. Withdraw eventually, stop being interested.* |
| *No one talks to me at activism meetings.* | Withdraw, *go home and watch TV, stop going to meetings.* |
| *People who get angry when I ask to register them.* | Attack, *yell,* "At least one of us cares about this country." *Quit registration drive.* |

Notice that Joaquin tends to use the same SCB for particular trigger categories. He attacks when he's criticized (except on a date, when he withdraws); he withdraws when he's excluded from a group; he surrenders when pressured to do something, and adopts a sullen, passive-aggressive demeanor. In his own words, here's what Joaquin learned from the worksheet:

## • *Example*

When I see the list of triggers and remember things that happened, I realize how often I am hurt—by criticism and whenever I feel left out, in particular. I see that what my schemas do when they are triggered is cause me tremendous pain.

The other thing I realize is how strong and automatic my reactions—the SCBs—are. I try to stop the hurt any way I can, usually by withdrawing to a safe distance—or by getting mad. I spend a lot of time being angry at people.

•

# Keep Learning about Your SCBs

Over the next week or two, stay alert in any interpersonal situation in which your schemas have been triggered before. Notice when schema emotions—hurt, anger, shame, and so on—get activated. Remember that any strong emotion you feel in reaction to others is likely schema driven.

Keep using your SCB Worksheet to record any triggering situations that occur, as well as the schema coping behavior you use to manage the pain. The point right now is to see what you do, not necessarily change what you do. Occasionally you may be able to respond to triggers in a different way from engaging in the old SCBs. That's good. But your old ways of coping are, by now, habitual, and it will take some time to change them.

# CHAPTER 5

# Schema Coping Behavior Outcomes

The last step of learning about your schema coping behaviors is to recognize specifically how they affect you and your relationships.

## Uncovering Your Schema Coping Behavior Outcomes

Every time you get triggered and every time you cope using an SCB, there are outcomes. Some of the outcomes will be emotional: You may be embarrassed by your behavior or afraid of how people may see you or react to you. You may feel more alone or depressed. Many outcomes are interpersonal—how others react to your SCB. In some cases, people may withdraw, get angry, cut you off, take advantage of your passivity, and so on.

---

### Exercise 5.1 Schema Coping Behavior Outcomes Worksheet

To explore schema coping behavior outcomes, look back at all the SCBs listed in your SCB Worksheet in the previous chapter. Now, in the following space, list the emotional and interpersonal outcomes for each schema coping behavior. What happened after you reacted—anywhere from an hour to a week later? What were your emotions about the event, and how did others respond to you?

# Schema Coping Behavior Outcomes Worksheet

| Schema Coping Behavior (from your SCB Worksheet in chapter 4) | My Emotions | Others' Reactions |
|---|---|---|
| 1. | | |
| 2. | | |
| 3. | | |
| 4. | | |
| 5. | | |
| 6. | | |
| 7. | | |
| 8. | | |
| 9. | | |
| 10. | | |
| 11. | | |
| 12. | | |

- *Example*

Hi, this is Joaquin again. Here's how I completed my SCB Outcomes Worksheet.

# Joaquin's SCB Outcomes Worksheet

| Schema Coping Behavior (from your SCB Worksheet in chapter 4) | My Emotions | Others' Reactions |
|---|---|---|
| 1. Withdraw, *refuse to talk to anybody (work)* | Depressed, alone | People ask what's wrong, then ignore me. |
| 2. Withdraw, *refuse to help on another project (work)* | Scared I may be in trouble at work | Coworker angry when I refuse involvement in another project. He walks away from me. |
| 3. Attack, *tell them it's bullshit (friends)* | Depressed, alone, uncared for | Generally people get angry back. Have lost two friends after these episodes. |
| 4. Surrender, *give in, get a little sullen (friends)* | Depressed, resentful | My needs are ignored. |
| 5. Withdraw, *stop calling people* Complain *about them to others (passive-aggressive) (friends)* | Depressed, alone | People stop calling me. A friend heard that I was complaining about him, and cut me off. |
| 6. Attack, *find something wrong with them (friends)* | Depressed, alone | People complain that I have no sense of humor, and tease me even more. |
| 7. Complain *to others, am cold and shut down if I see them (friends)* | Afraid I'm losing relationship | Relationship ends. |
| 8. Attack *("I can't find anybody who isn't like you") (mother)* | Hurt, dismissed | Mother gets mad and says horrible things, that I'm a failure. |
| 9. Withdraw, *refuse to talk (family)* | Depressed, alone | They ask me what's wrong, then continue to ignore me. |
| 10. Surrender, *give in, get sullen (mother)* | Depressed, resentful | Doing crap I hate to please her; she takes it for granted. |

| 11. | Withdraw, *stop talking (intimate relationship)* | Feel like a failure, disgusted with myself and with her | She seems to lose interest; won't return calls. |
|---|---|---|---|
| 12. | Surrender, *go along, try to be nice, eventually* Withdraw, *stop being interested (intimate relationship)* | Depressed, disinterested, alone | ? |
| 13. | Withdraw, *go home and watch TV, stop going to meetings (community)* | Depressed, alone | No one cares what I do. |
| 14. | Attack, *yell, "At least one of us cares about this country"; quit registration drive (community)* | No meaning, alone | They get angry; one person threatened me. |

Joaquin's SCBs are emotionally costly: he struggles with significant depression. And the more he withdraws or attacks, the more alone he feels. Both the attack and withdrawal SCBs are interpersonally damaging: Joaquin has lost two friends, and others avoid him.

Notice how SCBs often create outcomes that reinforce your original schemas. Joaquin's schemas were defectiveness/shame, social isolation/alienation, and self-sacrifice/subjugation. But as his SCBs cause him to lose friends and willing work colleagues, he slips deeper into feeling defective and alienated. And the belief that he must always please others grows stronger—because each rejection lowers his worth. This is the root of Joaquin's "alone" feeling: that people will always reject him because *there's something wrong with him*, something unacceptable.

SCBs are tragically self-perpetuating. The more you use them in relationships, the more people treat you in ways that confirm your schemas. This is one merry-go-round you want to get off.

SCBs are the root of your interpersonal problems. These reactions to schema pain are damaging your relationships and your life. Each time you attack, withdraw, or surrender in response to schema triggers, people around you get hurt and pull away. As your relationships get whipsawed with conflict, like Joaquin you may find yourself slipping into a sense of loss and alienation—and deep sadness.

There is a way out. The change process you'll learn in this workbook can alter the course of your life. Here's the first step.

# Stopping the Struggle

For much of your life, you've been trying to stop schema pain—and it hasn't worked. You've sought to get away from the situations and people that trigger you. And you've reacted with schema coping behaviors, expecting that schema feelings might somehow be blocked or minimized.

But you still get triggered; you still feel the fear or shame or sadness or hurt. For all this effort, the pain is still there and still gets activated. But not only does the schema pain persist; things also certainly get worse:

- You have lost relationships and become alienated from others.

- You may have lost jobs or the support of work colleagues.

- You may find yourself in painful conflicts, struggling over and over with people you want to be close to.

- You see the hurt and damage on the faces of those you love, people you wanted to protect.

- You may have lost a sense of belonging, even your self-respect.

- And through it all, the schema pain has grown worse, and those old negative beliefs about yourself seem stronger.

Here's the truth: trying to avoid schema pain by engaging in schema coping behaviors will not get rid of the pain. It will only make it deeper.

There are two kinds of pain: pain you can avoid and pain you can't. Schema pain can't be avoided. Perhaps you are beginning to see or suspect that now. When, by engaging in SCBs, you try to avoid unavoidable schema pain, it only makes it worse. The deepest kind of suffering in life derives from trying not to feel pain that has to be felt.

You grew up in a world that created your schemas; there's nothing you can do about that or the things that trigger you. What you *can* control is your response to the trigger. And that is what this book is about.

Schemas are like quicksand: the more you struggle and flail, the more trapped you become (Hayes and Smith 2005). Each time you withdraw, attack, or surrender, you sink deeper into schema pain. Each SCB damages your relationships and your feelings about yourself. Struggling with a schema, or trying to block or suppress it, is not the answer.

We are taught, if we get stuck in quicksand, to lie back and swim through the mush—not thrash in it. The same is true of schema pain. Swim through it; don't fight it.

One more analogy might be helpful. Schema pain is like the weather. All your feelings and thoughts are like the weather, moving across the sky (Harris 2009). Weather comes and goes. Sometimes you encounter thunder and rain, sometimes high-banked cumulus clouds, sometimes snow, and sometimes blazing sun. The weather keeps changing. You have sixty thousand thoughts a day and many, many emotions. If schema pain shows up, wait. It will change like the weather.

You are like the sky. You're what holds the weather, those ever-changing emotions. You don't have to fix your weather. Instead you can observe it, hold it, and let it be what it is until it changes.

# CHAPTER 6

# Mindfulness

This is the beginning of a radical change in how you respond to your maladaptive schemas and the painful emotions they trigger. The old way was to struggle, to fight the schemas and try to block the schema pain. But trying to avoid schema pain has only made it worse, while some of your relationships were lost or damaged in the process.

## Experiencing Mindfulness

The new way is to notice schema pain when something sets it off—and not try to stop or fix it. This ability to observe your experience without being driven to resist it can be a turning point in your relationships and your life. That's what we're going to work on now: strengthening your capacity to be mindful by simply watching sensations, emotions, and thoughts as they occur. It doesn't matter whether they are painful or pleasurable; you will learn to *just watch*.

---

## Exercise 6.1 The Five Senses

This mindfulness exercise is very relaxing and helps with focusing your mind on the present moment. It teaches how to attend to your senses one at a time so that you get skilled at noticing what you see, hear, feel, taste, and smell—right now. The exercise lasts two and a half minutes, and you are encouraged to notice as many experiences as possible while you focus on each of your senses.

You can record this exercise and play it back, or just read and follow each step.

## Sound: Thirty Seconds

*Bring your attention to the realm of sound. Notice what you're hearing right now. Be aware of ambient sounds—the hum of a refrigerator or air conditioner.... Are there voices, bird sounds, wind, the motor of a passing car?... Your own body may make sounds—as you move or breathe or swallow.... If your mind drifts or other thoughts come up, gently bring your attention back to what you're hearing.*

## Smell: Thirty Seconds

*Bring your attention to what you can smell.... Notice any fragrance or odor right now.... Inhale deeply and see if you can be aware of even the faintest smell.... If your mind drifts to other things, just bring it back to what your nose is telling you.*

## Sight: Thirty Seconds

*Now look around, observing colors and shapes.... Notice the largest objects...and the smallest details.... See things that are far away...and close by.... Just keep scanning and noticing what you see. If your mind drifts away to other thoughts, just bring it back to the realm of sight.... Just keep noticing everything you see.*

## Taste: Thirty Seconds

*Now notice what you can taste. There may be traces from things you recently drank or ate.... There may be a faint sense of sweet...or sour.... Lick your finger and notice the slight salty taste.... If your mind drifts to other things, just bring it back to sensations of taste.*

## Touch: Thirty Seconds

*Now notice sensations of touch.... Notice the temperature of the air.... Observe sensations of pressure or weight where your body touches the chair or floor.... Notice any textures, smooth or rough.... Notice what you feel inside your body—in your face or head...your shoulders and arms...your chest...your belly...your legs.... If your mind drifts away, just bring it back to what you feel.*

At the end of this exercise, check your level of relaxation. Did your mind race with thoughts, or were you mostly able to stay in the present moment? What was it like to notice your sensory experience in each realm?

---

This introductory mindfulness experience is the first step in strengthening your ability to observe the moment, experiencing whatever there is to experience without a lot of thinking or judging. Now we'll move on to the mindfulness skill of watching the breath and *labeling* experience.

---

# Exercise 6.2 Mindful Focusing

This exercise is a step toward *observing without struggling or resisting.* It will show you how to let passing thoughts and feelings have their moment and how to see them for what they are: temporary experiences that don't require you to *do* anything. You can record this exercise and play it back, or simply read and follow each step.

*Close your eyes and take a deep breath…and notice the experience of breathing. Observe perhaps the feeling of coolness as the breath passes the back of your nose or down the back of your throat…. And notice the sensation of your ribs expanding, the air entering your lungs…. And be aware of your diaphragm stretching with the breath, and of the feeling of release as you exhale.*

*Just keep watching your breath, letting your attention move along the path of flowing air…in and out…in and out. As you breathe, you will also notice other experiences. You may be aware of thoughts; when a thought comes up, just say to yourself,* Thought. *Just label it for what it is: Thought. And if you're aware of a sensation, whatever it is, just say to yourself,* Sensation. *And if you notice an emotion, just say to yourself,* Emotion. *Just label it for what it is: Emotion.*

*Try not to hold on to any experience. Just label it and let it go. And wait for the next experience. You are just watching your mind and body, labeling thoughts, sensations, emotions. If something feels painful, just note the pain and remain open to the next thing that comes up. Keep watching each experience, whatever it is, labeling it and letting it pass in order to be open for what comes next.*

*Let it all happen as you watch: thoughts…sensations…feelings. It's all just weather, while you are the sky. Just passing weather…to watch…and label…and let go.*

Meditate silently for another two minutes, and finish by opening your eyes and returning your attention to your surroundings.

We encourage you to do this mindful-focusing exercise daily so that you become more skilled at and more comfortable with observing your inner experiences.

---

After you've done mindful focusing several times, you may begin to notice some things. Labeling your inner experiences *thought*, *sensation*, or *emotion* helps you achieve some distance and increases your willingness to let even painful experiences run their course. More and more, you can learn to watch without judging or trying to stop what happens.

## • *Example*

My name is Arturo, and I'm a thirty-year-old legal aide. I have a lot of sadness—since my marriage ended. And when I do mindful focusing, it doesn't take long for it to show up. So I just say to myself, *There's an emotion.* Usually when I feel sad about her, I also get angry. And when I feel anger, I just say, *There's another emotion*, and when I have an angry thought, *There's a thought.* And here's the surprise: somehow I don't get all involved in it. I just *notice* it and then see what happens next, what else is going on. It's like, *Okay, I'm having this emotion—fine. And here's something else—fine.*

It's like going for a ride *inside yourself* and just watching the scenery. *There's a tree; there's a big rock.* You know what I mean? Watching but not getting all caught up in it.

•

# Mindful Activities

Mindfulness—the ability to observe each moment—isn't just about watching your inner experience. It's something you can learn through ordinary activities that you do every day. Instead of doing them in the usual distracted fashion, you can perform these tasks with full awareness. Here are some examples:

- *Mindful dishwashing:* Noticing the warm water, the slippery soap, the hard edges of dishes and utensils, the sound of the running tap

- *Mindful walking* (perhaps to and from work): Noticing the pressure of your steps (perhaps counting them); the sway of your hands; the shifting balance; the sights, sounds, and smells

- *Mindful gardening:* Noticing the cool feel of the soil, the tug while you are pulling weeds, the thrust of pushing in a trowel, the smell of flowers

- *Mindful bathing or showering:* Noticing the sound and feel of the water, the slippery soap, the shifting sensations as water sprays on various parts of your body

- *Mindful eating* (start with a snack or a light meal): Noticing the texture or temperature of the food, the smell and taste, the sensation of lifting a fork or spoon

- *Mindful drinking*: Noticing the liquid in your mouth, the temperature, the viscosity, the smell and taste, the feelings in your throat and stomach, the texture and weight of the glass or cup

The goal, of course, for mindful activities is to stay with your sensory experience. If thoughts or other private events come up, you can note them while returning your attention to your five senses.

Doing one or more mindful activities each day strengthens the skill of self-observation. It helps you learn to notice your experience—moment to moment—and to accept the experience for what it is, without judgment. We suggest starting with one or two mindful activities this next week, and committing to a specific time to do them. And then add one new activity each week thereafter until you are doing four to five mindfulness activities each day. Note that you don't need to take a lot of time with these activities. Rather, they are brief opportunities to be here, now.

- ## *Example*

I'm Linda, a forty-year-old preschool teacher. I was skeptical about whether mindfulness would be of any value to me. I chose mindful drinking as my first activity, using my morning coffee for the exercise. I began by simply holding the mug, feeling its warmth in my hands. Then I felt the steam on my face and noticed the aroma. As I began to drink, I felt the sensation of each sip, the sudden heat and bitter taste in my mouth.

Sometimes I'd lose concentration and start thinking of things I had to do that day. And I'd realize I had drifted off and then would go back to the smell and taste. I actually enjoyed the coffee more when I paid attention.

During the second week, I added a mindful shower and tried to mindfully walk the six blocks to the train. So I was doing these three mindful activities in the morning—and that's when I started to see a change. I was calmer and more aware at the same time. I was settled inside myself, yet super aware of what I was feeling and doing. I felt awake.

●

# Exercise 6.3 Mindful Talking

In this last mindfulness exercise, we'd like you to begin observing specific conversations. Choose one conversation you'd like to watch mindfully each day. The simplest way to do this is by making the choice in the morning—after thinking about whom you're likely to see in the next twelve hours. At this point, don't choose problem people or interactions where you might get upset. We'll work on that in the next chapter.

Here are the guidelines for mindful talking. While the conversation is underway, try to notice:

- Your thoughts (including judgments and assumptions about the other person)

- Your emotions (enjoyment, sadness, boredom, irritation, and so on)

- The other person's tone, posture, and facial expression

The goal of mindful talking is to observe the boundary or intersection between you and the other person. Your thoughts and feelings belong to you. They are reactions, not facts. They are just your experience. The facts are what you observe about tone, posture, and facial expression—and the literal words chosen by your conversational partner. The ways you interpret his or her words, tone, expression, and posture are your thoughts. They are not real or necessarily true; they live inside of you.

Each day, as you experience a few moments of mindful talking, separate what you observe using your senses from your private experience of thoughts and emotions. Knowing the difference between what you see and hear and what you think and feel can make a big shift in how you respond to people. More on that to come.

## • *Example*

I'm Rebecca. I'm forty-eight and I work in retail. I've struggled with anger toward my family. Here's what I noticed after experimenting with mindful talking for a week: I stayed away from doing this with problem people, but even so, I was getting irritated and was noticing a lot of thoughts about how people don't act right. There were a lot of judgments. And while this was going on, I noticed, on the other side, people smiling, having a friendly tone, just blathering away about something or other.

And I was feeling this chasm between what was going on inside of me and what seemed to actually be going on with these other people. It's as if there were two different conversations—the one they were having and the one in my head. And now, after a week of paying attention this way, I realize how often this happens.

•

# CHAPTER 7

# Observing Your Relationships Mindfully

Now it's time to begin using mindfulness skills to observe the relationships where you have problems. The key to changing what you do and how you react is to be fully aware at the moment you are triggered. Change is impossible, *choice* is impossible unless you can see exactly when the pain starts—before you are overwhelmed and lose control—and realize that you can do something new.

## Interactions That Trigger Schemas

The first step is to examine your current relationships and identify recurring interactions that trigger maladaptive schemas. The Interpersonal Triggers Worksheet will give you a chance to list the people—and their triggering behaviors—that launch you into schema pain.

## Exercise 7.1 Interpersonal Triggers Worksheet

To use this worksheet, begin by listing all the people who trigger strong emotional reactions. Think of the different domains of your life—work, family, children, partner, friends, and so on. Anyone who can set off feelings of shame, anger, guilt, fear, or sadness is likely triggering your schemas and should be listed in column 1, "Triggering People." Don't skimp on this—make as big a list as you can.

Now, in the right-hand column, list the things these people do to push your buttons. What actually is the behavior that offends or upsets you? List every triggering behavior you can think of, and be aware that some people can do more than one thing to precipitate schema pain.

# Interpersonal Triggers Worksheet

| Triggering People | Triggering Behaviors |
| --- | --- |
| 1. | |
| 2. | |
| 3. | |
| 4. | |
| 5. | |
| 6. | |
| 7. | |

## • *Example*

I'm Maggie, age forty-three. I struggle with very active abandonment/instability and defectiveness/shame schemas. Here's how I filled out the Interpersonal Triggers Worksheet:

| Triggering People | Triggering Behaviors |
|---|---|
| 1. *Boyfriend* | When he seems aloof; when he gets busy and can't schedule time together; when he gets angry about something; when he criticizes my parenting or how I manage my life |
| 2. *Mother* | When she criticizes my lifestyle; when she seems distracted or uninterested during our conversations |
| 3. *Ex-husband* | When he's cold or detached on the phone; when he criticizes my parenting decisions |
| 4. *Son* (age thirteen) | When he ignores me and shuts himself in his room; when I invite him to do things and he refuses; when he gets angry about my rules and how I run the house |
| 5. *The principal* (boss) | When she criticizes my lesson plans; monthly meetings where she points out problems |
| 6. *Parents* (of the children I teach) | When they complain about homework assignments, grades, problems in the classroom, and so on |
| 7. *Friend* | When she doesn't return my calls, when she criticizes my parenting (says my son is out of control); when she's late; when she talks about moving out of state |

Maggie will need to hone her observational skills in these triggering situations. And she'll need to be alert—with each of these people—for that moment when her old schema wounds get activated. Partly this involves planning ahead with the problematic individuals in her life:

- Remembering to observe what happens during her weekly call to her mother

- Being alert when she is picks her son from his weekends with her ex-husband

- Planning to watch her reactions during parent-teacher meetings

- Watching her responses during monthly meetings with the principal

- *Example*

Every one of the situations I listed can send me to the moon. The criticism, the feeling of not being cared for, the fear that someone's getting ready to leave—it all hits a nerve. And then I react. I get angry or I withdraw. Or with my son, I go overboard trying to please him.

None of that works, so I'm using the Interpersonal Triggers Worksheet to think ahead each day. Who will I have to deal with? Is this a problem person for me? Then, when I see that peraon, I try to stay alert, for moments when my schema buttons get pushed.

# Watching What Happens

As soon as your schema pain gets triggered and you see yourself starting to react, try to do one thing: *watch; don't act.* In other words, observe what's happening internally while trying *not* to get caught in schema coping behaviors. Here are things to watch:

- *Notice your schema-based feelings*—how the emotions wax and wane and sometimes morph into other feelings (hurt into anger, for example).

- *Notice your thoughts*—observing them come and go, while trying not to become too attached to any of them.

- *Notice your physical sensations*—feeling flushed or tense, and so on.

- *Notice impulses*—the urge to act and somehow avoid the schema pain. These are usually your SCBs.

- *Notice that you have a choice.* You can slip back into your traditional ways of coping—or not.

The *impulse* to act does not require action. The urge to engage in SCBs is not the same as the actual behaviors. As soon as the urge to act enters your awareness, try to recognize that there is a real decision possible: to do or not do what the mind and body urge.

# Learning from Your Observations

Keeping a diary of schema-triggering events will help you recognize the four components of schema pain:

- Schema emotions

- Schema-related thoughts

- Physical sensations

- Schema-driven urges

The diary will, after the fact, increase your ability to see and discriminate each part of the experience. During subsequent schema-triggering events, more importantly, what you learn from the diary will sharpen your observational skills. That's because you'll know what to look for. And you'll be more prepared to recognize the moment of choice—a time where you could decide *not* to act on schema-driven urges.

---

## Exercise 7.2 Interpersonal Experiences Diary

Fill out the Interpersonal Experiences Diary as soon as possible after each schema-triggering event. Certainly try to do it on the same day. Be sure to note whether or not you acted on schema urges.

# Interpersonal Experiences Diary

Event: _____

- Schema emotions: _____

- Schema-related thoughts: _____

- Physical sensations: _____

- Schema-driven urges: _____

Circle one:                    Acted on urge        Didn't act on urge

Result: _____

Event: _____

- Schema emotions: _____

- Schema-related thoughts: _____

- Physical sensations: _____

- Schema-driven urges: _____

Circle one:                    Acted on urge        Didn't act on urge

Result: _____

Event: _____

- Schema emotions: _____

- Schema-related thoughts: _____

- Physical sensations: _____

- Schema-driven urges: _____

Circle one:                    Acted on urge        Didn't act on urge

Result: _____


Event: _____

- Schema emotions: _____

- Schema-related thoughts: _____

- Physical sensations: _____

- Schema-driven urges: _____

Circle one:                    Acted on urge        Didn't act on urge

Result: _____

Event: _____

- Schema emotions: _____

- Schema-related thoughts: _____

- Physical sensations: _____

- Schema-driven urges: _____

Circle one:                   Acted on urge     Didn't act on urge

Result: _____

Event: _____

- Schema emotions: _____

- Schema-related thoughts: _____

- Physical sensations: _____

- Schema-driven urges: _____

Circle one:                   Acted on urge     Didn't act on urge

Result: _____

---

Your relationships have been affected—in some cases damaged or lost—when you have acted on schema-driven urges (used SCBs). As you've learned, the SCBs have offered temporary relief from the schema pain. But over and over, they have created conflict, even alienation, with the people who matter to you. That's why seeing the moment of choice is so important. Recognizing the urge and making a conscious decision will change your relationships.

- *Example*

I'm Jerry, a sergeant in a big-city police force. My schemas include mistrust/abuse and unrelenting standards/hypercriticalness. Here's a section of my Interpersonal Experiences Diary:

# Jerry's Interpersonal Experiences Diary

Event: *Patrolman fails to tape off crime scene.*_____

- Schema emotions: *Anger, anxiety*_____

- Schema-related thoughts: *He's stupid or He's lazy, nitwit, worthless, lost a lot of evidence*

- Physical sensations: *Tense gut, hot all over*_____

- Schema-driven urges: *Shout at him that he's incompetent.*_____

Circle one:          Acted on urge     (Didn't act on urge)

Event: *Wife demands that I discipline our daughter, who is quite angry because my wife yelled at her.*

- Schema emotions: *Anger*_____

- Schema-related thoughts: *She (wife) is setting me up. She's throwing me into a disaster of her own making. This is fucked up.*_____

- Physical sensations: *Feel hot, tight*_____

- Schema-driven urges: *Yell at her to clean up her own damned mess; don't dump it on me. I'm not going to have the same screwed-up relationship to our daughter as she has.*_

Circle one:          (Acted on urge)     Didn't act on urge

*Huge fight, daughter ran away*_____

Event: *Brother demands I pay half of costs for Mom and Dad's silver anniversary party.*____

- Schema emotions: *Anger, disgust*_____

- Schema-related thoughts: *He runs up this gigantic bill and wants to stick me with it; trying to screw me. He knows I can't afford this.*_____

- Physical sensations: *Hot, feeling of heaviness*_____

- Schema-driven urges: *I want to tell him I'm not going and I'm not paying for it either; it's bullshit and he can fuck himself.*_____

Circle one:     (Acted on urge)     Didn't act on urge

*Party canceled; we aren't talking.*_____

Event: *Mother calls about the party, says I disappointed Dad.*_____

- Schema emotions: *Guilt, anger*_____

- Schema-related thoughts: *I screwed up, wrong, bad. I'm damned if I'm going to be pressured into spending a ridiculous amount of money—she can pay for the damned party.*_

- Physical sensations: *Sick, almost nauseous, tight gut*_____

- Schema-driven urges: *Tell her to pay for it herself.*_____

Circle one:     Acted on urge     (Didn't act on urge)

My triggers tend to be situations where someone violates my standards or where I feel taken advantage of. My urge is always to get angry. Half the time I was able to resist the urge. These were situations where I was expected to be respectful. But with my wife and brother, I've had many upsets, and somehow I say whatever I feel like saying.

•

# Observing through Memory

As you've probably discovered, observation skills take time to develop. For one thing, when you get upset, it's hard to remember that you planned to watch your reactions. The resolve to observe yourself can go right out the window. Furthermore, schema-driven urges can come fast and furious, overwhelming your commitment to make a choice. Don't be discouraged when this happens. Your ability to mindfully observe triggering moments will improve with time.

Right now, there *is* something you can do to improve your observation skills. In the following exercise, you will visualize a recent triggering event and then observe (in memory) everything that happened. Choose an encounter that was emotionally upsetting. In the following script—which you can record or just read as you do the exercise—you'll be encouraged to see, hear, and feel everything that occurred. This will allow the emotion to build so that you actually have something to observe.

---

## Exercise 7.3 Practice Observing through Memory

Get into a comfortable position in a quiet place and close your eyes.

*Take a deep breath to release any tension in your body…. Take another deep breath…. Now return to a recent situation where you became upset, where your schemas got triggered…. When you have that scene in mind, try to see where you are; examine every detail of the situation and environment…. See who is there, what that person is doing…. Listen to what's being said, the tone of voice, the feel of the words…. Notice the temperature of your environment…the texture or sense of anything you touch.*

*Let your emotion build as you see the situation unfold, as you listen to what's said. Just watch and listen until your emotion is strong enough to observe…. As you watch this feeling, see if you can name the emotion. Just label the kind of emotion it is…. If there's more than one emotion, try to name the others as well.*

*Now pay attention to any thoughts that come up…. What are the thoughts that go with this situation?… What are the thoughts that go with this emotion?*

*Become aware of feelings in your body. What sensations go with your emotion? Notice the feelings in your face and head…arms…chest and abdomen…legs.*

*Now examine your schema-driven urges. What does the emotion make you want to do? Make you want to say?… Notice the strength of the urges and what happens as they rise in you…. Notice how you respond, whether you feel any choice or get swept along into the schema coping behavior.*

At the end of this exercise, record your emotions, thoughts, sensations, and urges in your Interpersonal Experiences Diary. Write them down, just as you would for any schema-triggering event.

We encourage you to do four to five "observing through memory" exercises. Write down the outcomes of each experience in your diary. Each time you do this exercise, you'll get more used to watching your schema-triggered reactions. The more you watch schema-triggering experiences from the past, the more effective you'll be at observing schema triggers as they occur in life. And the moment of choice, where you can make real changes in your relationships, becomes increasingly apparent.

---

In the week ahead, there are likely to be several opportunities to observe your schema feelings, thoughts, and urges. If you commit to observing these experiences, there will be moments of surprising clarity—woven among times when you forget everything. That's okay. The ability to change how you respond isn't an on-off switch. It's a gradual—two steps forward, one step back—evolution in your relationship choices.

Remember the analogy of the sky, the weather? You are learning to watch the weather rolling across your sky. The mindfulness skills in this chapter will increasingly (1) give you the choice to watch rather than act, and (2) help you become the sky—holding an experience rather than being driven by it.

The old helplessness, where you felt forced to react to every schema-triggering event, will no longer define you. Instead, you can stand at a distance, watching people trigger you, watching your emotions and urges, and still feel a sense of choice. Emotions won't govern your behavior; you—the person who decides what matters in your life—will choose what you do.

# CHAPTER 8

# Values

So far you have identified your maladaptive interpersonal schemas and the painful feelings they generate. You've had a chance to observe how your thoughts and feelings arise in different interpersonal situations. And you've explored how these negative thoughts and feelings lead to the same action urges over and over.

You are probably starting to notice moments of choice, like the times when someone criticizes you and you start to feel really bad about yourself. And you feel the moment of decision between blowing up and taking some other course. Those same old feelings keep coming up and you feel the urge to withdraw, attack, deflect your attention, or use whatever schema coping behavior you have used in the past—the same old actions that you don't want to take anymore.

You might also have noticed that it's not enough to vow that you *will never do* something again. That leaves a behavioral vacuum and often fails. You need to plan alternative behaviors—positive things you can do that will replace your old ways of coping with people. That's what this chapter is all about: creating a plan for real, successful behavior change.

## Core Relationship Values

The first step in successful behavior change is to clarify your relationship values. What is most important to you in your relationship with your parents, your partner, your kids, your friends, your boss? Your schemas may tell you that the most important thing is being right or avoiding criticism, but deeper down, your better self has other, more positive and powerful values, such as honesty, love, or respect. These bedrock values are the engine of successful behavior change.

To uncover and clarify your core relationship values, you'll explore these six domains:

- Work relationships

- Friendships

- Family

- Parenting

- Partner relationships

- Community relationships

Values are the direction you want to go in life, not specific goals you want to achieve. For example, you might want your daughter to get her driver's license. That's a goal. The underlying values are your commitment to being supportive of your daughter's becoming a more independent person. Or you might want to help a friend paint her kitchen. That's a goal that can be accomplished, and then it's done. The value is being someone your friends can count on for help, which persists over time and establishes a direction you consistently travel throughout your life. The individual goals—picking your old college roommate up at the airport, loaning a friend your car, taking a boring class that a friend is teaching—are like milestones or signposts along the way. They are indications that you're on the right road.

---

# Exercise 8.1 Values Domains Worksheet

For each of the following domains, rate its importance to you, using this scale:

0—Not important

1—Somewhat important

2—Very important

Then in the next column, write your value in each domain. Use your own words to describe the way you want to be with people in your life.

Finally, write down your behavioral intention. This is some specific action you can take that would be motivated by your value and would express it. The intention helps you become more of the person you want to be in that relationship. Or it allows the relationship to grow in ways that you value.

# Values Domains Worksheet

| Domain | Importance 0–2 | Value | Behavioral Intention |
|---|---|---|---|
| Work Relationships | | | |
| Friendships | | | |
| Family | | | |
| Parenting | | | |
| Partner Relationships | | | |
| Community Relationships | | | |

## • *Example*

I'm Rebecca. I'm a thirty-six-year-old assistant office manager at a large property-management company. I was married for six years, but now I'm divorced and I'm dating a guy who's a little younger than I am. I don't have any kids. Here's how I filled out my Values Domains Worksheet:

## Rebecca's Values Domains Worksheet

| Domain | Importance 0–2 | Value | Behavioral Intention |
|---|---|---|---|
| Work Relationships | 2 | *Give honest (not mean) feedback.* *Support coworkers' creativity.* | *Honestly but gently say what I think about our new software project.* *Take each new idea seriously and find a positive aspect to praise.* |
| Friendships | 2 | *Be a caring friend.* | *Instead of withdrawing, make contact with friends at least once per week.* |
| Family | 1 | *Be a loving, supportive daughter.* | *Rather than focusing on what I wish she were, praise Mom in each phone call about something that I appreciate.* |
| Parenting | 0 | | |
| Partner Relationships | 2 | *Be a loving, supportive girlfriend.* | *Instead of focusing on things to criticize, look for one thing each day to appreciate out loud.* |
| Community Relationships | 1 | *Help kids in my community.* | *Apply to be a "Big Sister" and follow through by participating in the training.* |

All of my values center on loving, caring for, and supporting others. But so often I don't act on that. I'm too critical and negative, and I look for flaws in others and their ideas. So you'll notice that I started most of my behavioral intentions with "Rather than…" or "Instead of…" I was trying to remind myself that when I feel that Mom or my boyfriend, David, is stupid or irrational, I don't have to be critical or sarcastic. I can choose to act on my deeper values and find something to do or say that is more caring and supportive. This exercise was a big eye-opener for me.

•

## • *Example*

My name is Kyle. I'm thirty-two years old. I have two kids, ages eight and six; my wife left me a year ago; and I'm stuck in a dead-end job. You can see my worksheet below.

## Kyle's Values Domains Worksheet

| Domain | Importance 0–2 | Value | Behavioral Intention |
|---|---|---|---|
| Work Relationships | 1 | Reliability, honesty | Stop calling in sick; put in an honest day's work for my pay |
| Friendships | 2 | Trustworthiness | Pay Johnny back the money I owe, or do a work exchange |
| Family | 0 | | |
| Parenting | 2 | Be a steady, dependable dad | Plan fun, appropriate activities for my weekends with the kids |
| Partner Relationships | 1 | Stay friends with my wife, Becky, and her family | Make support payments on time, help maintain the house |
| Community Relationships | 1 | Be a worthwhile member of society, somebody who gives back | Help out at school fundraisers and spring trip |

I would say that I really have good values but don't act on them enough. I'm more likely to act on my feeling that there is something wrong with me, something that keeps me from showing up at work on time, making child-support payments, or doing fun things with my kids. Writing down the behavioral intentions made it clear how somebody should act who supposedly has the values I say I have.

•

# Values-Based Behaviors vs. Schema Coping Behaviors

Your behavioral intentions can become values-based behaviors that eventually replace the schema coping behaviors that you have used to avoid difficult interpersonal situations. Instead of damaging your relationships, your behavior can foster and improve them.

---

## Exercise 8.2 New Intentions Worksheet

Refer back to your schema coping behaviors from the SCB Worksheet in chapter 4. Use the first two columns of the following worksheet to write down your schema coping behaviors in various domains. Then use the last two columns to summarize your values and intentions for behavior that can replace your old schema coping behaviors.

# New Intentions Worksheet

| Relationship | Old Schema Coping Behavior | Value | Intention |
|---|---|---|---|
|  |  |  |  |
|  |  |  |  |
|  |  |  |  |
|  |  |  |  |

- *Example*

Hello, my name is Anne. I'm a fifty-one-year-old tax accountant. I used the New Intentions Worksheet to figure out replacement behaviors for how I used to behave in my relationship with my mother and her family. Here's how I filled it out:

## New Intentions Worksheet

| Relationship | Old Schema Coping Behavior | Value | Intention |
|---|---|---|---|
| *Mother* | *Attack* | *Be loving* | *Explain that she hurt me; set limits in a kind way.* |
| *Mom's family* | *Withdraw* | *Be connected and close* | *Take an interest in people—join a conversation and ask people questions about themselves.* |

In the next chapter, you'll learn how to develop the willingness to experience some schema pain in order to put your values into action.

# CHAPTER 9

# Willingness

In this chapter you will start replacing some of your old schema coping behaviors with your new values-based behaviors. You'll try out your new behaviors and track your progress. You should see your problem relationships gradually improve. That's the good news.

The bad news is what is likely to happen when you stop acting according to your schemas: the painful feelings that your schemas are designed to avoid will inevitably come up. You will probably experience some of the anxiety, depression, anger, and so on that led you to develop your schema coping behaviors in the first place.

There is no way to escape or entirely eliminate these painful feelings. The only option, if you are to live according to your values, is to accept the feelings and be willing to feel them. That's why this chapter is titled "Willingness."

## Measuring Your Progress Weekly

Keeping track of your values-based intentions is important. It helps motivate you, even when you are facing difficult schema emotions.

---

### Exercise 9.1 Values Compass

Here is one good way to rate your progress. Review your behavioral intentions from the previous chapter, and act on them during the week. At the end of the week, imagine that each of the following six circles is a compass and that, instead of pointing to north, it points to your values.

For each of the domains of your life, draw an arrow representing how well you have moved in the direction of your values.

| Work Relationships | Values |
|---|---|
| | (circle with center dot) |
| Friendships | Values |
| | (circle with center dot) |
| Family | Values |
| | (circle with center dot) |
| Parenting | Values |
| | (circle with center dot) |
| Partner Relationships | Values |
| | (circle with center dot) |
| Community Relationships | Values |
| | (circle with center dot) |

For example, if you did everything you intended to do in your relationship with your parents, you would draw an arrow pointing straight up to your values. If you failed in every opportunity to take your intended action, your arrow would point straight down, away from your values. If you were successful about half the time, your arrow would point to the right or left.

| Family | Values |
|--------|--------|
|        |        |

| Family | Values |
|--------|--------|
|        |        |

| Family | Values |
|--------|--------|
|        |        |

### • *Example*

Hi, this is Rebecca again. The first week I tried to put my values into action, I had trouble following through on my good intentions. Each day I would vow to be positive and affirming in my relationship with David, and then I'd usually fall back into my old critical remarks. On Tuesday he wore a stained shirt to dinner with my mother, and I blasted him for it, when it was a perfect opportunity to express my appreciation for the fact that he was missing a basketball game on TV so that he could eat out with us. I did a little better on Thursday, when I told him how much I appreciated his enthusiasm for working on our garden, even though I didn't think he had dug the vegetable bed deep enough. But then on Friday, he complained about my work schedule, which made me feel like a failure, and I slipped back into criticizing him to protect myself.

I noticed that the same feelings of failure and embarrassment kept me from being supportive of David. I thought my mother could see what a callow slob he was, and I thought that our whole backyard would be a disastrous failure. Overall, my "Partner" compass for the week looked like this:

| Partner Relationships | Values |
|---|---|
| | |

## Exercise 9.2 Weekly Rating

If the compass format doesn't appeal to you, keep track of your progress toward your values with a simple scale from 0 to 10, where 0 means that you made no progress at all and 10 indicates that you succeeded at every opportunity to put your values into action:

| Domain | Rating 0–10 |
|---|---|
| Work Relationships | |
| Friendships | |
| Family | |
| Parenting | |
| Partner Relationships | |
| Community Relationships | |

# Commitment vs. Barriers

Your behavioral intentions are a commitment to yourself to do what matters, to be who you want to be in your relationships. A commitment to your values is no less sacred than a promise to someone you love. It is saying, "I will do _____ because it is important, because my old schema coping behaviors are damaging my relations and I don't want to live like that anymore."

It helps to share this commitment with others. Tell your friends and loved ones, your therapist, and even your coworkers (if that is appropriate). Making a formal and public commitment increases the power of your commitment and your chance of success.

As you struggle to live up to your commitment to yourself, you are likely to face some barriers. The barriers can be primarily emotional, as when Rebecca's feelings of failure and embarrassment kept her from supporting her boyfriend. Or the barriers can be cognitive: thoughts about the difficulty of change or past failures, for instance.

### • *Example*

My name is Ruthy. I'm twenty-three years old. My intention was to finally tell my friend Janice that I took credit for some of her work in our computer-graphics class last semester. My barriers were some really strong, bad feelings. I was ashamed that I had stolen her ideas, and I felt even guiltier that I didn't cop to it right away. And then there was the feeling of just being not as smart or diligent as Janice, being too dull and uncreative and lazy to develop my own concepts.

### • *Example*

My name is Jack. I'm sixty-three. When I retired, my intention was to uphold my value of being an equal partner with my wife, Joan. I wanted to help out with the cooking, cleaning, and household budgeting. The barriers to that were mostly cognitive: I thought I was a pretty old dog to be learning new husband tricks. Over the years I vowed to cook at least one meal a week or to repair things around the house, and I never quite got those things done. Joan has been carrying more than her share of the domestic load for years, and I really doubted my ability to take over things that I had little aptitude for or interest in.

## Exercise 9.3 Assessing Barriers Worksheet

Barriers are easier to overcome when you know your enemy, when you articulate and analyze the barriers. Use the following Assessing Barriers Worksheet to identify the behavioral intentions you are having trouble with and the nature of the barriers to accomplishing those intentions.

## Assessing Barriers Worksheet

| Behavioral Intention | Emotional Barrier | Cognitive Barrier |
|---|---|---|
| 1. | | |
| 2. | | |
| 3. | | |
| 4. | | |
| 5. | | |
| 6. | | |
| 7. | | |
| 8. | | |

- *Example*

Hello, this is Rebecca again. Here is how I filled out my Assessing Barriers Worksheet for my relationships with my coworkers and my mom. First I imagined how I would carry out each intention. I totally visualized the scene and watched what feelings and thoughts came up. Finally I wrote short descriptions of what I learned.

## Assessing Barriers Worksheet

| Behavioral Intention | Emotional Barrier | Cognitive Barrier |
|---|---|---|
| 1. *Honestly and gently say what I think about our new software project.* | *Aftraid of change and failure* | *Safer to be against it now so that if it fails, I won't be blamed. This project is stupid.* |
| 2. *Take coworkers' ideas seriously and find positive aspects to praise.* | *Ashamed, defensive, inferior* | *They might really be smarter than I am. Praising them puts me one-down.* |
| 3. *Rather than focusing on what I wish she were, praise Mom about something I appreciate during each phone call.* | *Resentful* | *She's selfish. She says things to make me feel small.* |

These barriers, especially the emotional ones, were very intense for me. But writing them down helped me see that it was my own negativity that was holding me back, keeping me from connecting with my mom or people at work in any meaningful way. They weren't putting the barriers in my way; I was.

●

The cognitive barriers are usually judgments or "what if" thoughts about danger. Rebecca's were both, and they served to intensify her fear and resentment. And—this is what makes barriers so difficult—the more Rebecca's thoughts fueled her emotions, the harder it was for her to act on her values.

# Exercise 9.4 Monsters on the Bus

Steven Hayes, the creator of acceptance and commitment therapy, likes to use the metaphor of a bus to illustrate the way that barriers can block committed action (Hayes, Strosahl, and Wilson 1999; Hayes 2005):

*Imagine that you're driving a bus called "Your Life." On the front of the bus is a sign saying where the bus is headed. The sign is a value, like "Being a loving person" or "Doing what I say I'm going to do."*

*When you turn the bus in the direction of your values, barriers arise in the form of painful emotions and thoughts. They pop up in front of you like monsters. You can't drive around them or run them over. You could stop the bus and wait for them to go away, and that's exactly what you do every time you put valued actions on hold because of painful thoughts or emotions. Unfortunately, those monsters don't go away, so your bus is stalled by the side of the road.*

*Suppose that instead of stopping, you turn away from the monsters/barriers? You head in a different direction, far from your values. You drive to the land of SCBs, schema coping behaviors, where all you care about is stopping painful thoughts and feelings. But the SCBs create their own pain. They damage and destroy your relationships.*

*The solution? You have to let the monsters on the bus and take them along for the ride. They'll continue to try to cause trouble, yelling from the back of the bus that the route you're taking is too dangerous, scary, dumb, difficult, and so on. They'll make you sad or scared or angry. That's what monsters do. That's their job. Your job is to keep driving the bus in the direction that you've chosen.*

Committed action requires willingness on your part to feel some painful emotions in service of your values. Your values are your motivation. Focusing on the destination posted on the front of your bus helps you keep driving, no matter what the monsters do or how much emotional noise they make.

## • *Example*

Hi, this is Rebecca again. I imagined that I was at work, driving the bus of my life toward my value of being more honest and supportive of my colleagues. My intention at a particular meeting about the new software was to explain my concerns gently and honestly, without harshly sniping at others' ideas, which is my usual mode of operation.

Anyway, the first monster that popped up was fear of looking stupid or incompetent. If I admitted that the software had some positive features and that the people in favor of it had some good ideas, then I might seem not as smart as they are, not so innovative.

That was bad enough, but then this second monster popped up: distrust and suspicion. I had the thought that these other people at work would walk all over me to get to the top, that it was a fight to the death, that if I let down my guard for a moment, I'd end up laid off and living in a Dumpster.

The third monster was the worst: I felt that it wasn't just professional competition that set others against me. I felt that they didn't like me and I didn't like them. I could see what was going to happen. These three monsters would stop my bus dead at the side of the road. Or worse, I'd turn in the direction of the SCBs. I'd start all my usual defensive sniping, sarcastic put-downs, opposition to anybody else's ideas. I could see past the current meeting to the future, when they would finally decide that it was easier to fire me than to constantly fight with me.

During that meeting I was quieter than usual—a little less negative when I did speak, a tiny bit more positive. To complete the metaphor, I let the monsters onto the bus. I inched the bus a little bit forward, toward my goal of honesty and support instead of criticism and opposition. And all the time, the monsters in the back of the bus were screaming: *You'll be a failure, You'll be fired, People don't like you, They'll hurt you.* And I could feel the fear, believe me.

Eventually I was able to let the monsters on the bus sooner, with less time spent stuck in the ditch. I realized that if I take them with me, I can go where I want to go.

•

Rebecca's work situation is a good example of a major theme in acceptance and commitment therapy: choosing between avoidance and facing pain while living your values. The fact is you're going to have painful feelings in life. You can have them and be stuck, or you can have them while pursuing your goals according to your core values.

## • *Example*

My name is Jeanie. I'm thirty-seven years old. When I think about my bus, I see "Forgiveness via Compassion" on the front. I want to drive toward reconciliation with my father and my stepsister, Sylvia. My dad left us when I was nineteen, and when my mom remarried, I got a new stepsister with whom I never got along. Now that we're all older, family is more important to me, and I want good relations with my dad and Sylvia. But I do have those monsters that pop up in front of the bus. My monsters say things like: *Dad never cared for you as he should, so why should you give him the time of day now? Sylvia's a sneaky bitch, and you can't trust her. If you open up to her, she'll take advantage somehow.* When I listen to these monsters, I drive off course. I avoid my family—I don't return their phone calls and e-mails. I withdraw into my work and my dogs and my wine. I have to let the monsters onto the bus. I have to hear those old messages of resentment and yearning and anger, but keep driving straight ahead.

●

# Awareness Going Forward

Whenever you choose to act on your values, watch what happens:

- Observe and mentally label the emotional barriers that make you want to avoid acting on your values: fear, shame, sadness, loss, anger, and so on.

- Observe the cognitive barriers as well: thoughts of danger and judgments about yourself or others.

- As much as possible, hold on to a willingness to experience whatever thoughts and feelings arise, while still acting on your values.

- Write down these observations if it helps you to remember keep acting on your values while being willing to experience some uncomfortable feelings and thoughts.

# CHAPTER 10

# Defusion: Watching, Labeling, and Letting Go of Thoughts

In this chapter, you will learn how to handle the alarming thoughts that inevitably come up when you try to act in relationships according to your true values. When you stop letting your anxiety or anger determine how you interact with people, and instead put values like trust or community in charge, your old schema thoughts will no doubt be triggered. You'll find yourself thinking:

*This won't work; I can't do this.*

*He doesn't love me.*

*She's selfish and doesn't care about me.*

*They'll see how screwed up I am.*

*I'll be rejected.*

*Everybody leaves me in the end.*

*She will hurt me.*

*I can't do anything right.*

*If I'm honest, he'll be disgusted.*

Sound familiar?

# Types of Schema-Driven Thoughts

Schema-driven thoughts tend to fall into three categories:

**Predictions.** You look into a crystal ball and see a future clouded by your fears and doubts. For example, Marjory predicted that if she confessed to her boyfriend, Bryan, that she found his lovemaking unimaginative and dull, he would think she was a kinky freak, be disgusted, and leave her. Raoul repeatedly turned down his uncle Jorge's offer of a better job, predicting that he would fail to live up to expectations and thus let his family down. Shelly stayed in her dorm room night after night, skipping all the campus social activities because of her prediction that she would do or say something stupid and be ridiculed.

**Memories.** You look backward through that same crystal ball and see a past full of losses and failures. For example, Clare always left meetings and other events as quickly as she could, instead of lingering to chat with people, because of her memories of feeling awkward and tongue-tied in such situations. Larry went to the gym religiously, but never talked to the other people there, remembering painful interactions that went all the way back to the locker room in high school. Betty started taking a community-education class in line dancing, but dropped out because it reminded her too much of mixers in college, where she felt weird and out of place.

**Negative judgments.** Your crystal ball tells you, without evidence and yet without doubt, that you or others are incompetent, selfish, uninterested, and so on. For example, Danielle found something wrong with every guy who ever asked her out: "too short," "too bald," "too fat," "too loud." Rich hated his bookkeeping job, but he didn't apply to any other firms because of his judgments of one company as too stodgy and conservative, another as using unsound accounting practices, and a third as too high pressure and greed driven. Claudia knew she should give her kids positive feedback and unconditional love, but she couldn't stop putting labels on them: "stupid," "lazy," "sneaky," "stubborn."

# How Your Mind Works

Thoughts occur spontaneously. You have little control over their content. You have little control over how often they come up. Schema thoughts are going to pop up from time to time, whatever you do. But if you are trying to act differently in your relationships, according to your newly clarified values, then schema thoughts are absolutely going to pop up—frequently and vividly. For example, if you are prone to schema thoughts about abandonment and your new friend cancels a date, this minor rejection will be sure to trigger all your old thoughts about people leaving you forever.

To become more aware of how your mind generates these schema thoughts, it helps to think of your mind metaphorically, in terms of real-world objects or experiences that it resembles:

**A popcorn machine.** Your mind functions like a popcorn machine, popping up thoughts one after another Hayes, Strosahl, and Wilson 1999). Sometimes a whole lot of thoughts pop in rapid succession. Sometimes the rate is slower, with isolated thoughts here and there, separated by brief moments of silence. But your mind never stops entirely. And you can't turn off the popcorn machine of your mind. And you can't speed it up or slow it down. Your mind just keeps popping up thoughts: pop, pop, kernel after kernel. That's how it's designed. That's how it works.

**A tug-of-war fanatic.** Your mind loves to play tug-of-war (Hayes, et al. 1999). When schema thoughts come up, it's as if your mind were handing you one end of a rope and challenging you to a tug-of-war. Trying to resist or argue with your schema thoughts is like grabbing the rope and starting to pull. The harder you pull, the harder your mind pulls back. As you continue to try to refute the schema thought or turn it off, you are digging in your heels and pulling harder and harder on the rope, making your mind also dig in and pull back harder, in the form of more negative judgments, more rotten memories, more dire predictions.

The way out is to let go of the rope. Stop pulling and just drop it. The way to "handle" painful schema thoughts is not to "handle" them at all; just let them go, even the most painful and disturbing ones. Every effort at control is just picking up the rope and returning to the tug-of-war. When a painful thought occurs, you have a real choice to make about how to respond. You can do one of three things: attempt to suppress or refute the thought, buy into the thought and agree with it, or notice it and let it go. The attempt to suppress or refute the thought is like picking up the rope, while noticing the thought and letting it go is like dropping the rope.

**A pushy sales rep.** Picture your thoughts as sales representatives (Vuille 2006). Mundane, everyday thoughts are like polite salespeople who offer you something you don't care for very much and then go away quietly if you don't express interest. On the other hand, schema thoughts are like high pressure, pushy salespeople who are peddling tempting luxury products. They hang around you and keep trying to entice you with a suitcase full of products. If you say okay and give them your attention, very quickly the suitcase is open and stuff is spread out all over your living room. If you buy one product—buy into one schema thought—suddenly the rep has a bunch of other things to sell you.

This metaphor gets at three key concepts: first, some thoughts are more compelling than others. The more compelling thoughts are closely connected to your oldest and strongest negative schemas about yourself and others. They grab your attention like a model in a designer dress or rich, savory food or a sleek luxury car. They are very attractive, despite the fact that you can't afford them and they're not good for you. Second, buying into one schema thought is likely to trigger a whole chain of related thoughts, opening the pushy sales rep's suitcase. Third and most important: the metaphor reminds you that you have a choice. Buy-in is not automatic. You can buy the schema thought or not. You can give schema thoughts significant attention and serious consideration, or you can let them go. One of the best ways of letting them go is cognitive defusion.

# Cognitive Defusion

*Cognitive defusion* is a term coined by Steven Hayes, founder of acceptance and commitment therapy (Hayes, Strosahl, and Wilson 1999). He noticed that people become "fused" to their negative thoughts. They become so firmly attached to their thoughts that they think they *are* their thoughts. He developed exercises to teach people how to "defuse" from their thoughts and see themselves as *having*, rather than *being*, their thoughts.

Defusion is related to the Buddhist practice of observing and distancing from thoughts. Many of the defusion exercises are similar to Buddhist meditation practices in which you observe, label, and then let go of intrusive thoughts.

Cognitive defusion has four component skills:

1. Watching thoughts

2. Labeling thoughts

3. Letting go of thoughts

4. Distancing from thoughts

In this chapter we'll offer a variety of exercises and thought experiments, all adapted from McKay et al., 2011, and some based on Hayes et al., 1999, to help develop each component skill.

# *Watching Exercises*

The following two exercises are all about pure observation: just watching as your mind entertains one thought after another. They will begin to show you how the mind works as an automatic thought-generating machine.

---

## Exercise 10.1 White Room Meditation

Find a quiet place where you won't be disturbed for five to ten minutes. Lie down or sit down, with your arms and legs uncrossed. Close your eyes and take a few deep, slow, calming breaths.

*Imagine that you are in a white room, completely empty of furniture or any adornments. You can position yourself anywhere in the room: at the ceiling, on the floor, or in one of the corners. But wherever you put yourself, visualize an open doorway to your left and a second open doorway to your right. The doors give onto darkness; you can't see anything beyond them.*

*Now imagine that your thoughts are entering from the doorway on your left, passing across your field of vision, and exiting through the doorway on your right. As your thoughts cross the room, you can attach them to a visual image of a bird flying, an animal running, a hulking mafioso, a balloon, a cloud, or anything else. Or you can simply say the word "thought" to yourself. Don't analyze or explore your thoughts. Let them each have a brief moment in your awareness and then exit through the doorway to your right.*

*Some thoughts may feel urgent or compelling and stick around longer than others. Just let them move on out the door to make room for the next thought. As new thoughts show up, make sure you've relinquished the old ones, but don't worry if the old ones show up again. Lots of thoughts tend to repeat themselves, and the visitors to your white room may be no exception.*

Continue the exercise for five to ten minutes, and then remind yourself of your actual surroundings and open your eyes. How was the exercise? Did you notice that the pace of your thinking changed? Did the thoughts eventually come slower or faster? How easy or hard was it to let go of a current thought to make room for the next thought?

---

If you enjoyed the previous exercise, keep doing it as often as you wish. Or move on and try "Mindful Focusing."

---

# Exercise 10.2 Mindful Focusing

This is a version of the Buddhist practice of meditation. Find a quiet place where you won't be disturbed for five to ten minutes. Lie down or sit down, with your arms and legs uncrossed. Close your eyes and take a few deep, slow, calming breaths.

*As you continue to breathe deeply and slowly, notice your breath. Notice the feeling of the cool air washing over the back of your throat, down your windpipe, and into your lungs. Notice the feeling of your ribs expanding and contracting, and notice your diaphragm tensing and releasing as you let go of a breath. Keep observing your breathing and noticing each part of the physical experience.*

*Take this opportunity, as you notice the experience of your breath, to be aware of what your mind is doing. As each thought comes up, label it,* There's a thought, *and return your attention to your breath. Just breathe, acknowledge the thought, and return to awareness of breathing. Remember that you don't need to pay a lot of attention to each thought. Your attention should continually return to your breathing. Experts in meditation say that it is this repeated refocusing of attention—from breathing to distracting thought and back to breathing—that is the essence of meditation, the source of its power and beneficial effects.*

Continue the exercise for five to ten minutes, and then remind yourself of your actual surroundings and open your eyes. How was the exercise? Did you find that the pace of your thinking changed? Were some thoughts harder to let go of than others?

For at least two weeks, do five minutes of mindful focusing each day. If you enjoy the exercise, of course, you can spend more time focusing. Over the course of the next two weeks, notice any changes in your relationship to your thoughts. Is there any shift in terms of intensity, believability, or intrusiveness?

---

# *Labeling Techniques*

The following two practices are really techniques instead of exercises, because you do them on the fly, as needed. Using these techniques, you can begin to put a name to each thought, a process that will gradually make two things clear: that your thoughts are just thoughts, separate from yourself and not automatically true, and that your thoughts tend to repeat the same themes over and over.

---

# Exercise 10.3 "I'm Having the Thought…"

These four simple words are like magic. They make you take a step back from your thoughts and get a little distance from them. Here's how it works: when you notice that you're worrying or brooding over something, rephrase each thought in your mind by putting *I'm having the thought that…* on the front end.

---

## • *Example*

My name is Todd. I'm thirty-two years old. I was obsessing about my girlfriend, Linda, possibly leaving me. Then I remembered the "I'm having the thought…" technique, so I began rewording my thoughts like this:

*I'm having the thought that Linda is going to leave me. I'll come home one night—no, I'm having the thought that I'll come home one night and she'll be gone. I'm having the thought that I'll fall apart. I'll start drink—I'm having the thought that I'll start drinking again and I'll spiral down. I'm having the thought that I'll spiral down into a dark pit. I'm having the thought that no one will ever love me again.*

I found that inserting the phrase *I'm having the thought…* made me slow down my thinking. It made me separate my thoughts into shorter statements and showed me that I had at least three different trains of thought going on: how lonely I would be, my drinking, and future relationships. Most importantly, this technique reminded me that Linda *hasn't left me yet*. It was all speculation, all catastrophic thinking taking place in my mind, not out in objective reality.

•

## Exercise 10.4 "Now My Mind Is…"

This defusion skill uses labeling to emphasize that thoughts are products of the mind, not *a priori* truths. Practicing the skill is simple. Just memorize the phrase "Now my mind is having the thought…" and use it to describe whatever thoughts arise when you are worrying or ruminating about some situation in your relationships. The neat thing about this formulation is that it can be altered slightly to categorize your thoughts. You can use the form, "Now my mind is having a _____ thought."

- ### *Example*

I'm Celia. I'm thirty-eight years old. I used "Now my mind is…" to expand my thoughts and reword them like this:

*Unlovable. Now my mind is having the thought that I'm unlovable. Now my mind is having the thought that there's something wrong with me. I'm damaged—I mean, now my mind is having the thought that I'm damaged goods. Now my mind is having the thought that it will always be like this; I'm doomed, or rather, now my mind is having the thought that I'm doomed.*

When I started using this form, I began to feel some distance between my "self" and my thoughts. I understood what they mean about *observing* your thoughts instead of *being* your thoughts. As I got better at this technique, I started putting my thoughts in categories, like this:

*Now my mind is having an* I'm unlovable *thought. Something's wrong with me—now my mind is having a judgmental thought. Damaged—now my mind is having a regretful thought. Now my mind is having a pessimistic thought. Doomed—now my mind is having a* doomed *thought.*

Whenever you start to feel depressed or anxious about your relationships, remember that you now have these labeling techniques. You can defuse from the depressing or anxious thoughts by rewording them and categorizing them. Here are some more examples:

| Schema Thought | Defused Thought |
|---|---|
| *She hates me.* | *I'm having the thought that she hates me.* |
| *This will never work.* | *I'm having the thought that this will never work.* |
| *It's hopeless. Why bother?* | *My mind is having a hopeless thought.* |
| *They're jerks. To hell with them.* | *My mind is having an angry thought.* |

# *Letting-Go Exercises*

The following are visualization exercises that give you many images or metaphors to represent letting thoughts go. They are a good way to learn how to let "sticky" thoughts leave your mind instead of sticking around. Try each one and experiment with them to see which works best for you.

## Exercise 10.5 Leaves in a Stream

Find a quiet place where you won't be disturbed for five to ten minutes. Lie down or sit down, with your arms and legs uncrossed. Close your eyes and take a few deep, slow, calming breaths.

*Imagine that you are on the bank of a stream in autumn. As each thought arises in your mind, see it as an autumn leaf that falls from the trees into the fast-moving stream. Watch the thought/leaf hit the water, swirl around in the current, and get swept downstream, disappearing around a bend. As each new thought appears, turn it into a leaf and let the stream carry it away.*

Continue the exercise for five to ten minutes, and then remind yourself of your actual surroundings and open your eyes. How was the exercise? Did you find that the pace of your thinking changed? Were some leaves harder to let go of than others?

## Exercise 10.6 Billboards

Find a quiet place where you won't be disturbed for five to ten minutes. Lie down or sit down, with your arms and legs uncrossed. Close your eyes and take a few deep, slow, calming breaths.

*Imagine that you are in a car, driving or riding down a stretch of highway. As thoughts show up, visualize them as if they were on a billboard that gradually gets larger as you approach and then disappears behind you. Each new thought becomes a new billboard, sweeping into your awareness and then disappearing in a flash.*

Continue the exercise for five to ten minutes, and then remind yourself of your actual surroundings and open your eyes. How was the exercise? Did you find that the car speeded up or slowed down? Were some billboards hard to pass, or did duplicate billboards show up?

## Exercise 10.7 Balloons and Clouds

Find a quiet place where you won't be disturbed for five to ten minutes. Lie down or sit down, with your arms and legs uncrossed. Close your eyes and take a few deep, slow, calming breaths.

*Imagine that you are holding a bunch of helium-filled balloons on strings. Or imagine that you are watching a clown who's holding such a bunch of balloons. As each thought enters your mind, put it on a balloon and let go of the string. Watch the balloon rise up into the sky until it is a tiny dot that then disappears: new thought, new balloon to let go of. Alternatively, you could place your thoughts on clouds forming in the sky and drifting away over the horizon.*

Continue the exercise for five to ten minutes, and then remind yourself of your actual surroundings and open your eyes. How was the exercise? Did you find that the pace of your thinking changed? Did some balloons or clouds want to stick around?

## Exercise 10.8 Computer Pop-Ups

Find a quiet place where you won't be disturbed for five to ten minutes. Lie down or sit down, with your arms and legs uncrossed. Close your eyes and take a few deep, slow, calming breaths.

*Imagine that you are sitting in front of your computer, looking at a picture of a peaceful nature scene. See each of your thoughts as a pop-up advertisement that suddenly appears superimposed over your screen. Click on the "X" in the corner of each pop-up to make it disappear.*

Continue the exercise for five to ten minutes, and then remind yourself of your actual surroundings and open your eyes. How was the exercise? Did you find that the pace of the pop-ups increased or slowed? Were some pop-ups likely to appear several times?

## Exercise 10.9 Trains and Boats

Find a quiet place where you won't be disturbed for five to ten minutes. Lie down or sit down, with your arms and legs uncrossed. Close your eyes and take a few deep, slow, calming breaths.

*Imagine that you are in your car, stopped at a railroad crossing, watching a long freight train grind past. See the dusty boxcars and hear the rhythmic clanking of the wheels on the tracks. As each thought enters your mind, put it on a boxcar and watch it go past and away. If you don't like the train imagery, try visualizing a river with boats cruising past.*

Continue the exercise for five to ten minutes, and then remind yourself of your actual surroundings and open your eyes. How was the exercise? Did you find that the train speeded up or slowed down? Did some boxcars just stall in the intersection and sit there for a while? Or did the same thought/boxcar/boat go by several times?

## Exercise 10.10 Physically Letting Go

Here's one you can do with your eyes open. Sit up straight and hold your dominant hand out in front of you at a comfortable level, palm turned up. As a thought occurs to you, imagine that it is in the palm of your hand. When the thought is firmly in hand, rotate your hand to the palm-down position, and imagine the thought dropping away into oblivion. Turn your hand palm-up again and wait for the next thought. Keep "dropping" or "letting go" of each thought as it appears. By performing the physical motion of letting go, you can make the experience of letting go of thoughts feel more real and concrete.

How do you find this exercise? How fast do new thoughts come up? Do the same thoughts come up over and over?

You can do this exercise at any time, to reinforce your defusion of troublesome thoughts. If you are self-conscious about making these gestures in public, you can replace the hand-turning with a very subtle movement of your wrist, a slight spreading of your fingers, or a gentle lifting of your fingers as if waving good-bye.

---

## Watching, Labeling, and Letting Go All at Once

Pick your favorite watching exercise, your favorite labeling technique, and your favorite letting-go exercise, and combine them as a single exercise. For your convenience, here is a list of all the exercises in this chapter:

- Watching Exercises
  - Exercise 10.1 White Room Meditation
  - Exercise 10.2 Mindful Focusing

- Labeling Techniques
  - Exercise 10.3 "I'm Having the Thought…"
  - Exercise 10.4 "Now My Mind Is…"

- Letting-Go Exercises
  - Exercise 10.5 Leaves in a Stream
  - Exercise 10.6 Billboards
  - Exercise 10.7 Balloons and Clouds
  - Exercise 10.8 Computer Pop-Ups
  - Exercise 10.9 Trains and Boats
  - Exercise 10.10 Physically Letting Go

Make a point of doing this practice several times a day, at specific times, such as before getting out of bed, while riding the bus, during your lunch hour, on a walk, and so on. At many of these times, you won't be able to lie down and close your eyes, but you can still do the watching exercises in your imagination, while walking around with your eyes open.

Likewise, don't wait for your worst schema thoughts to come up. Practice watching, labeling, and letting go of whatever thoughts are in your mind in the moment, even if they are neutral or pleasant thoughts, like what to have for dinner or what to name your new cat.

## • *Example*

My name is Carol, and I'm a twenty-nine-year-old customer-service rep at a restaurant-equipment company. Last year I signed up with a dating website, looking for a new boyfriend. The whole online-dating experience really brought up all my old schemas. I combined watching, thought labeling, and letting go of thoughts to help me manage my feelings.

I started with the "White Room Meditation" while lying on my couch with my eyes closed, imagining a white room with two doors. I found that my negative thoughts about dating easily took the form of different types of men entering the room by one door and leaving by the other door. There were three particular types of guys that appeared several times, in slight variations: a handsome guy who sneered at me, an ugly guy who leered at me, and a really creepy guy.

It was pretty obvious that these figures represented my main fears about online dating: that the really good-looking guys will never choose me, that only the ugly ones will want me, and that some creepy pervert might show up. It was hard for me to let go of these thoughts, hard to get those guys to leave the "white room."

Next I started using the labeling techniques. When I thought about handsome guys not choosing me, I rephrased my thoughts like this: *Now my mind is having a low–self-esteem thought.* When I thought about only being able to attract ugly men, I responded with, *Now I'm having a "poor me" thought.* When I started worrying about meeting creepy people, I told myself, *Now my mind is making another dire prediction.* Putting this different spin on my thoughts helped me see that they were just thoughts. I can get a little distance from my thinking and realize that nothing has happened yet. I am just sitting up in here spinning my mental wheels.

I made a coffee date with a plumbing contractor I met online. Before the date I tried one of the letting-go exercises. When a downer thought occurred to me, like *This will never work,* I held my right hand out palm-up and imagined the thought was in my hand like a nasty little dust bunny, and then I turned my hand over and let the thought drop. During the date itself, I had the thought, *He looks at least ten years older than his picture.* I put my hand under the table and made the palm-dumping gesture to help me let go of the thought and return my attention to what the guy was saying.

All together, I must have gone on ten coffee dates, sometimes followed by a dinner date with the same guy. It was difficult sometimes, but I got a lot out of my defusion techniques. They helped me keep enough distance from my negative thinking to keep going out and doing what I said I would do: put myself out there in the dating scene.

Finally I met Greg—a not bad looking, genuinely nice guy who actually likes me and thinks I'm funny. We're still together today.

●

The defusion skills you learned in this chapter can be tremendously helpful when schema-driven thoughts get in the way of new intentions. Rather than letting these thoughts derail you, you can use defusion, which provides ways to simply watch your thoughts.

# CHAPTER 11

# Defusion: Distancing

In this chapter you will continue learning defusion exercises. The ones in this chapter are distancing exercises that will help you create space between your "self" and your thoughts, as well as help you take your thoughts less seriously.

## The Paradox of Defusion

All these exercises share a common element: in doing them you acknowledge, accept, and even *embrace* painful thoughts while paradoxically letting them diminish in importance. You'll see how it works as you try out each of the following distancing exercises. Experiment with each one and discover which ones work best for you.

---

## Exercise 11.1 "Thank You, Mind"

Your mind is always busy, working every moment to do its main job, which is to help you survive. Your mind is always on the lookout for danger and more than willing to point it out to you. Your mind is constantly making judgments about what's good or bad for you. Your mind keeps up a running commentary on events to try to explain why everything that happens to you happens.

Like an overprotective, domineering parent, your mind can go overboard. Your mind can be hypervigilant and see danger where there really is none. Your mind can be hypercritical and make way too many harsh, painful, negative judgments. Your mind can go on and on, explaining events in a way that makes you feel ashamed or stupid or crazy. In other words, your mind keeps repeating the negative schemas that you know so well.

You can move away from an overprotective parent, but you can't move away from your mind. You can't really silence or ignore your mind either—not really, not for long. But you can thank your mind. It sounds so simple and trivial, but it works like magic. Just try it.

When your mind presents a painful schema thought for your consideration, inviting you to buy into it and entertain it for an extended time, use this mantra:

*Thank you, Mind, for that thought.*

And let it go. Whatever your mind comes back with, again say to yourself, *Thank you, Mind, for that thought*, acknowledging the schema thought, accepting it graciously with thanks, but not arguing or discussing (Hayes 2005). It's like mental martial arts. You move *with* your mind's attack, not against it, not resisting and trying to stop the thought. "Thank you, Mind" sidesteps the thought, letting your mind's momentum carry the thought past you and away.

You can combine "Thank you, Mind" with labeling and string together a long series of these elegant responses: *Thank you, Mind, for that "fear" thought; Thank you, Mind, for that "I'm bad" thought; Thank you, Mind, for that judgmental thought.*

---

## •   *Example*

My name is George. I'm forty-six years old. When I tried the "Thank You, Mind" technique, I was thinking that my boss wanted to fire me. If you could have read my mind like the dialogue in a script, here's how it would have sounded:

MIND. He has it in for me.

GEORGE. Thank you, Mind, for that thought.

MIND. Better start looking for a new job; I'm toast here.

GEORGE. Thank you, Mind, for that discouraging thought.

MIND. The boss said, "Good Morning," in a very bored tone. He's decided to fire me already.

GEORGE. Thank you, Mind, for that catastrophic prediction.

MIND. I keep messing up and he knows it.

GEORGE. Thank you, Mind, for that thought too.

It looks a little strange written out this way, but the effect on me was profound. Saying *Thank you, Mind* allowed me to stop spending all my time at work worrying about my boss's opinion of me. I actually was able to spend more time doing my job, and I started to receive better performance evaluations.

•

## Exercise 11.2 Negative-Label Repetition

This technique is also called "Titchener's Repetition," based on pioneering psychologist Edward Titchener's discovery (1910) that repeating any word fifty or more times tends to rob it of all meaning. Even very disturbing words or phrases, the ones that sum up your most painful schemas, lose most of their punch with repetition.

Try it for yourself. Pick one to three words that sum up your most horrible thought monster, the schema thought that most plagues you. Really try to boil the monster down to a single word. Here are some examples of words that other people have come up with:

*selfish*

*hurtful and mean*

*bad husband*

*loser*

*unlovable*

Negative-label repetition couldn't be simpler. Just say your word or phrase over and over for at least a full minute. Say it out loud, clearly, rapidly, and at a fairly loud volume. Afterward, examine what has happened to the meaning of the word or phrase. Does it feel somewhat devoid of meaning, more like a sound than a word? If so, use this technique any time you are experiencing schema thoughts and your situation allows you to talk like this without appearing like a complete nut.

● *Example*

I'm Christina, thirty-one years old. I used negative-label repetition to defuse from my thoughts about my weight and my husband, Jim. I kept thinking, *Jim's not attracted to me anymore. I got too fat. I've seen him looking at Liz; she's still so slim. I'm way overweight compared to her; Jim says it doesn't matter, but it does—no one really loves a fat girl.* The theme of my thinking was pretty clear. I summed up all my thoughts easily in one word: "fat."

One night when I got home from work, I sat in my car in the garage, where no one could hear me. I said, "Fat, fat, fat, fat, fat, fat, fat, fat!" over and over for about a minute and a half, really loud. It felt really silly at first, but by the end, I was smiling. The word had become almost pure noise to me. I really felt more detached and less upset.

●

## Exercise 11.3 Physicalizing Thoughts

You can shrink the power of thought monsters by physicalizing them (Hayes 2005). *Physicalizing* means giving the thought a particular color, size, shape, and texture. By doing this, you turn the thought into an image or a metaphor and gain distance from the thought. Use this form to try physicalizing one of your schema thoughts:

Schema thought: _____

    Color: _____

    Size: _____

    Shape: _____

    Texture: _____

● *Example*

My name is Sheila. I'm fifty-five years old. I used physicalizing to gain distance from one of my angry, suspicious thoughts about the people at work. Here is what I wrote:

Schema thought: *They're all against me, lying to me.*

Color: *Sickly, puke green*

Size: *Vast, like Lake Michigan*

Shape: *Round and flat, like a giant pancake, but very thin*

Texture: *Slick, like glass*

I created a vivid image of my anger and suspicion as a vast plate of sickly green glass floating in the sky above me. It helped me let go of the thoughts, because if the giant plate was in the sky, it wasn't in me. I could imagine it floating farther and farther away instead of pressing in on me.

---

# Exercise 11.4 Card Carrying

This exercise gets the thoughts out of your head and onto a card that you carry with you (Hayes 2005). Get a 3 by 5 index card and put it in your wallet or purse so that you'll have it with you as you go about your daily routine. When a particularly troubling thought occurs to you, write it down on the card. When the thought returns, tell yourself, *I don't have to think about this; it's on the card.*

---

## • *Example*

I'm Brian. I'm twenty-two years old. I used the card-carrying technique after a weekend vacation trip with my new girlfriend, Sally. I had been nervous about everything going smoothly and our having the perfect time. Whenever Sally seemed distracted or quiet, I had thoughts that she was bored or angry with me. I worried about spending too much or too little money, wanting to give just the right impression of being neither a cheapskate nor a spendthrift. I tried to keep a conversation going every moment, which led me to blurt out some things about my business and my old girlfriend that perhaps would have been better left unsaid.

On Monday my mind was rehashing the weekend so constantly that I couldn't concentrate on work. Monday night and Tuesday I carried an index card around. Here is what my card looked like by Tuesday night:

| |
|---|
| *I'm boring.* |
| *Talked too much.* |
| *Stupid about money.* |
| *Offended her somehow.* |
| *She thinks I'm weird.* |
| *She'll dump me.* |
| *Blabbermouth.* |
| *Seafood restaurant was a mistake.* |

Having this card in my wallet helped me defuse from my schema thoughts about my unworthiness and ineptness around women in general, and Sally in particular.

●

# Exercise 11.5 Wearing Signs

This exercise combines aspects of card carrying and negative-label repetition in a particularly effective way. In the privacy of your own home or room, write one of your typical negative self-judgments on a sticky note and stick it to your chest or arm where you can see it. As you go about your normal activities, you'll notice the sticky note from time to time. The note and its negative message gradually become commonplace, less startling, and less upsetting. Putting the negative judgment on the note gives you some distance from it, like card carrying; and noticing it over and over robs it of power and meaning, like negative-label repetition.

## • *Example*

I am Susie and I'm forty-three years old. I had been beating myself up about not visiting my family more often and not helping out more with my stepsister's wedding. I wrote "Selfish" on a sticky note and stuck it on my stomach. I wore it all day Saturday, when I was at home, scrubbing down my kitchen cabinets. The note kept falling off, so I had to stop and pin it to my T-shirt with a safety pin. By 5:00 p.m. the kitchen was spotless, I was exhausted, and I took the note off and looked at it for the hundredth time. I could not have defined "Selfish" without a dictionary, and I had stopped obsessing so much about my family.

●

---

# Exercise 11.6 Four Key Questions

This is an exercise to do when you have some experience with the previous exercises and have identified your most persistent schemas: the thoughts that plague you, the thoughts that return time after time, despite all the card carrying and "Thank you, Mind"—the thoughts that keep you from having the kind of relationships you really want (McKay, et al. 2011).

Remember the bus metaphor—how the thought monsters pop up in front of your bus and try to get you to change direction, away from where your values lead? When you are dealing with a recurring, persistent thought monster like *I'm unlovable* or *There's something wrong with me*, it helps to ask yourself these four key questions:

1.  *How old is this thought?* Think back and remember the earliest age at which you had this thought. How old were you? What was going on in your life back then?

2.  *What's the function of this thought?* What is your mind trying to achieve? Keeping you safe? Saving face? Most schema-driven thoughts, even the most painful, are designed to help you avoid some other kind of emotional pain. If you are unlovable, perhaps that means you don't have to try for love and experience the pain of failure. If there is something wrong with you, maybe that means you are not responsible for your mistakes and don't have to feel guilty. What bad feeling does this thought protect you from?

3.  *How's the thought working out for me?* Thought monsters tend to cause more pain than they protect you from. What has your thought done for you, really? How has it warped and stunted your relationships over time?

4.  *Am I willing to have this thought and still act on my values in relationships?* Here's the payoff, the real money question. Are you willing to let this thought monster on the bus and keep driving in the direction *you* want to go, despite the monster's ravings from the back of the bus? If your answer is yes, what is a concrete thing you could do or say to someone that comes right out of your values?

Try it now with one of your own schema thoughts. In the following space, write down your recurring thought and your answers to the four questions.

# Four Key Questions

**Thought:** _____

1.  *How old is this thought?* _____

_____

_____

_____

2.  *What's the function of this thought?* _____

_____

_____

_____

3.  *How's the thought working out for me?* _____

_____

_____

_____

4.  *Am I willing to have this thought and still act on my values in relationships?* (What will you do or say?)_____

_____

_____

_____

- *Example*

I'm Corinne, a twenty-six-year-old warehouse clerk. I filled out the "Four Key Questions" like this:

## Corinne's Responses to the Four Key Questions

**Thought:** *No one really cares about me, about what I go through.*_____

1. *How old is this thought? Eighteen years, since I was eight, with Mom yelling at us kids and my brother crying all the time.*

2. *What's the function of this thought? Keeps me from being hurt by Mom's anger, by my brother's constant complaining about his rotten childhood. Mine was just as rotten, but he doesn't care, doesn't even hear me.*

3. *How's the thought working out for me? Made me withdraw from my brother. Kept me lonely and hurt even worse all these years.*

4. *Am I willing to have this thought and still act on my values in relationships?* (What will you do or say?) *Yes. Next time my brother complains, I'll listen and connect with him. I won't shut down and go cold.*

Two weeks after doing this exercise, I saw my brother at our cousin's wedding. I spent a long time at his table, listening closely to his old complaints about our mom. My thought monster whispered in my ear, *He only cares about himself. He doesn't care about me.* But I had an old business card in my clutch purse with "Nobody cares" written on it.

I said back to the monster, *Thank you, Mind, but I've already got that on the card.* I managed to keep listening to my brother, really hearing him for the first time in years. Since I was not withdrawing and retreating as usual, my brother did not have to put so much energy into arguing to get me to come around to his point of view. He cut his chronic complaining short, and by the time the cake was cut, we were laughing about our rotten childhood together.

●

# Exercise 11.7 Combo Defusion

Now that you have many defusion techniques in your arsenal, from both this chapter and the previous chapter, you can put them all together and have some fun with index cards. Get about ten index cards and write one of your typical schema thoughts on each one. Shuffle the cards and then turn up the first card. Defuse the message on that card using one of the defusion techniques you have learned. Keep reshuffling and turning up cards at random until you can defuse the thoughts quickly and automatically.

- ## *Example*

My name is Frank. I'm sixty-one years old. I tried the combo-defusion exercise with eight cards. Here is one of my sequences, written out like a script:

Card.    You're being so cruel to tell your girlfriend about things that bother you in the relationship.

Frank.    Thank you, Mind, for that thought.

Card.    You're being very inconsiderate of others' feelings.

Frank.    I'm having a judgment thought.

Card.    She's going to get sick of you.

Frank.    I'm having the thought that she's going to get sick of me. It's just a thought.

Card.    You have to realize how selfish you're being. If you don't, nobody will want to be around you.

Frank.    (opening his hand) I hear that thought, and now I'm letting it fall away.

Card.    She's probably already mad at you.

Frank.    I'll let that one go too. It's drifting away—a silly red balloon.

Card.    You're too demanding.

Frank.    That's an old thought. My mother used to say it. All it's doing is trying to shut me up.

*Card.* You're just going around hurting people, and then you'll be alone.

*Frank.* Thanks, Mind, for the judgment and the fear thought.

*Card.* She won't put up with you much longer.

*Frank.* (turning his hand palm-down) Another fear thought—letting go, letting go.

●

# The Observer Self

What do all these defusion techniques have in common? They are ways to detach: to detach your "self" from your experience, to detach your "self" from your thoughts, and to detach your "self" from your feelings.

Sometimes your "self"—the essential you—gets merged with thoughts and feelings. You have the judgment *I am bad*, as if that were you, as if your "self" were bad. That's fused thinking: the thought and the self seem like the same thing. This contrasts with defusion, where you say, *I'm having the thought that I'm bad*. And you and the thought are not the same.

You can also get merged with feelings. *I'm afraid* makes it seem as if you were the fear, as if fear were part of the core you. That's different from noticing that, at this moment, you feel afraid, which is a passing emotion that does not define you. See how having a feeling of fear contrasts with *I'm afraid*? When you have a feeling of fear, you are observing something that will change and pass. It isn't you. When you are afraid, you are the fear.

Thoughts and feelings constantly change, and you are the one who watches them come and go. This watcher is the observing "self." Can you experience being the observer? As thoughts and feelings come and go, there is still this "you" noticing. See if you can be aware of this observer self, this person behind your eyes who watches what you think, what you feel, what you do. If you observe your worst self-judging thought, then you aren't the same as that judgment. You are watching. You aren't your thoughts, feelings, or sensations. You are the one who observes, notices, and holds all these things.

Many parts of you have changed over the years. You've gotten older, your thoughts and feelings have constantly changed, and you've learned things and now see some things differently than you did before. But your observer self has always been there, never changing. See if you can sense this deeper you.

## The Movie-Screen Metaphor

One way to think about the observer self is to imagine that your immutable, unchanging self is a movie screen (Hayes 2005). Every day a new movie plays on the screen—tragedies, comedies, adventures, love stories—all of them full of emotions like loss and hope, laughter and fear. The movies are full of ever-changing dialogue (your thoughts). Although the movie, with its emotions and dialogue, constantly changes, the screen is always there, just the same.

What movie has been playing on your screen today? What part of the movie is playing right this moment? For a little while, right now, sit back and be the screen. Review the actions of the day, and hear your thoughts and feelings like a soundtrack of dialogue and music. Everything on the screen is moving and changing, but the self, the observer self, never changes.

## The Chessboard Metaphor

Here's another way to visualize the observer self. Imagine a game of chess in which the pieces are thoughts and feelings (Hayes 2005). The white thoughts and feelings are at war with the black thoughts and feelings. The interactions are complex and totally absorbing to the players. Eventually white wins or black wins, and the game is over. The board is cleared and the players start another game. Instead of being a piece on the board, instead of being a player, be the board. Visualize yourself as the board on which all the conflict and strategy are played out. The board is the observer self, and when each game is over, the board remains.

As the board, you can *have* the pieces. You can be in contact with the pieces, those black or white thoughts, those black or white feelings. But whether there are more black or white pieces on the board at any time, the board never changes. The board stays the same. It doesn't care about the game, about who wins or loses. From the space of being the board, you can hold all the pieces, experience them, and yet not *be* them.

For your convenience, here is a list of the skills covered in this chapter:

- Defusion Exercises
  - Exercise 11.1 "Thank You, Mind"
  - Exercise 11.2 Negative-Label Repetition
  - Exercise 11.3 Physicalizing Thoughts
  - Exercise 11.4 Card Carrying
  - Exercise 11.5 Wearing Signs

- Exercise 11.6 Four Key Questions

  *How old is this thought?*

  *What's the function of this thought?*

  *How's the thought working out for me?*

  *Am I willing to have this thought and still act on my values in relationships?*

- Exercise 11.7 Combo Defusion

- The Observer Self

- The Movie-Screen Metaphor

- The Chessboard Metaphor

# CHAPTER 12

# Facing Schema Emotions

You're now well acquainted with the emotional pain that maladaptive schemas stir up. Avoiding that pain, by using schema coping behaviors, has negatively affected your relationships and your life. It's time to learn to observe and accept schema pain—without being driven into your old SCBs. To achieve this, we'll present a technique called "exposure." Instead of avoiding schema emotions, you'll learn to face them in a time-limited, structured exercise.

Exposure will help you in the following ways:

- You'll learn to *watch* the schema emotion instead of lurching into an avoidance response.

- You'll get used to the emotion rather than feel so afraid of it. And when the emotion isn't so scary, you'll be less driven to engage in SCBs.

- You'll notice that emotions are time limited, showing up in a wavelike pattern as they intensify, crest, and then slowly subside.

- You'll learn to accept the emotion as part of your current "weather," knowing that it will change soon enough.

## Why Exposure Helps

There are three things people do that intensify and prolong painful emotions: try to stop or avoid the emotion, act on the emotion, and ruminate about the emotion. You know all about trying to avoid schema emotions with SCBs—in the end it makes things worse. Acting on the emotion (attacking when you're angry, running away when you're afraid) also strengthens the feelings. Research (Tavris 1989; Linehan 1993) shows that the more you engage in emotion-driven behavior, the stronger and more enduring the emotion becomes. Similarly, *thinking* about why you feel the way you do, judging yourself, or imagining bad things that might happen intensifies schema emotions. The more you ruminate, the worse you feel.

Exposure exercises teach you to watch what you feel without avoidance, emotion-driven behavior, or rumination. So they help you *not* do the things that make emotions worse. Instead, you observe what you feel until it changes or passes, learning to accept the experience for what it is.

---

# Exercise 12.1 Emotion Exposure

You can do this emotion-exposure exercise in two ways: as emotions actually get triggered in everyday life, or using imagery to trigger emotions from recent upsetting events. Because it's more challenging to do exposure as emotions are triggered in the moment, we recommend that you learn how to do it using the image of a recent upsetting event.

You can record and play back the following exposure script, or simply read it, a section at a time, while doing the exercise.

1.  Recall a recent schema-triggering event.

    *Go back to the moment when that schema pain was triggered. Notice your surroundings; notice who is there and what that person looks like.... Now listen to any sounds that go with the scene, such as background noises or voices; listen to what is being said that upsets you.... If someone's behavior or demeanor upsets you, become aware of that.... Keep watching the scene and listening to what's said until you feel—right now—the schema emotion.*

2.  Notice sensations in your body.

    *Observe your physical sensations; what do you feel in your body? ... Scan your body to see where the feelings are.... Imagine that the sensation has a shape and size—what would it be? ... Imagine that it has a color—what would the color be? ... What is the sensation like—a knot, a weight, a feeling of pressure?*

3.  Notice the schema emotion.

    *Observe the emotion that goes with that upsetting scene.... Describe it to yourself; describe its intensity and quality.... Is it sharp or dull? ... Could you imagine the emotion having a size...shape...color...texture? As you watch, see if the emotion changes in intensity or morphs in any way.... Describe to yourself what you notice.*

4.  Notice and label your thoughts.

    *As thoughts come up, just notice and label them. Say,* There's a thought. *And then let it go. You don't have to get involved with it or follow where it leads. Just say,* There's a thought.... *If you have a judgment—about yourself or another—just notice it and let it go. After noticing each thought, go back to observing your emotion and describing it to yourself. Describe whether it is changing in any way.*

5.  Notice action urges.

    *Observe any impulse to do something.... See if the emotion is pushing you to take action.... Just be aware of the urge without doing or saying anything.... Let yourself watch without acting.*

6.  Notice blocking urges.

    *Be aware now of any need to block the emotion, to push it away. But just keep describing to yourself what you feel.... Just stay with the feeling, noticing any changes. Is the emotion stronger? Less strong?... Notice where you are on the wave: ascending, cresting, receding? Are other emotions beginning to weave themselves in?*

7.  Stay with the exposure.

    *Again notice the sensations in your body—where they are and what they feel like... and then notice your emotions and describe them to yourself.... If you have a thought, say,* There's a thought *and let it go. Just return to watching and describing your emotions.... If you have an impulse to avoid your feelings, notice it and return to watching the emotions.... If you have an impulse to say or do something, notice it and return to your feeling.... If the emotion is changing, let it change.... Just keep watching until the emotion changes in some way.*

Here is a summary of the key steps for emotion exposure:

1.  Visualize a recent schema-triggering situation. (Skip this step for emotions that you are observing in the moment.)

2.  Notice how you feel inside your body.

3.  Observe your emotion, describe it to yourself, and notice if the emotion is growing or diminishing.

4.  Notice, label, and let go of any thoughts; return to the emotion.

5.  Notice action urges; return to describing your emotion.

6.  Notice blocking urges; return to describing your emotion.

7.  Stay with the exposure, describing the emotion and watching the waves until the emotion changes.

We encourage you to do emotion exposure for brief periods at first—five minutes or less—stopping even if the intensity of the emotion doesn't change. Get used to it. It takes a number of brief exposures before you feel more acceptance and a greater sense of *allowing* when schema pain arises.

As you get more comfortable with observing and feeling schema emotions, extend the exposure sessions so that you can actually watch these feelings change. At this point you can also begin doing present-moment exposure—when you are still suffering from a triggering situation. Here's how. As soon as your schemas get activated, do the following:

1.  Notice and resist the urge to engage in SCBs.

2.  Take a break from the triggering situation as soon as possible.

3.  Observe your emotions. Stay with them until you feel able to accept, rather than resist, these feelings.

4.  Recall the specific intentions you have for values-based behavior in this relationship.

5.  Make a plan to act on your intentions.

The key for present-moment exposure is to keep observing your feelings until you have enough *acceptance* to act on your values—not return to old SCBs. This is why exposure is so important. It builds the psychological muscle—called willingness—that gives you choice. When you are confident, you can feel whatever schema emotion shows up; you're no longer driven to avoid. Instead you can choose a values-based response.

## •   *Example*

My name is Lara. I'm often triggered by Jane, who has the workstation next to mine. She's always boasting about how fast she gets everything done, and she acts surprised if I have to work late—as if I'm stupid or inefficient. Her remarks always hit my "failure" button.

I started practicing exposure by imagining recent things she had said, like the time she claimed to have done her sales report in an hour and acted surprised that mine took longer. I got a mental image of her all prim and full of herself at her desk. I could hear the mocking surprise in her voice: "Are you still doing that report, Lara?" I was angry in a second—as I always am.

So I watched what was happening in my body (a knot in my stomach, a flushed face) and then described the emotion to myself. The anger was like a wall of rage, and then I saw beneath it this sick, incompetent feeling, this feeling that I don't know what I'm doing.

I watched my thoughts—I had a lot of judgment thoughts about her and then myself. So I just kept saying *thought* or *judgment thought* and tried to get back to watching my emotions. Sometimes it was hard to let go of the judgments, but eventually I got my focus back on the feelings.

I noticed urges to say something angry or catty. I noticed my mind trying to avoid the whole thing by thinking about my vacation. But as soon as I caught myself avoiding, I got back to my feelings.

So I just kept trying to describe the anger and the incompetent feeling. During the first few exposures, the feeling didn't change. But when I pushed them a little longer, I noticed the feelings dying down a little. I was on the back end of the wave.

●

Notice that Lara was struggling with more than one schema-driven emotion. The core emotion was feeling like a failure, but the anger acted as a cover, an avoidance of deep feelings of incompetence. Whenever anger is the triggered emotion, check to see if there are emotions underneath that the anger is suppressing.

Lara, as is common, didn't notice much change in her emotions in the first, brief exposures. But when she increased her exposures, she began to notice the emotional intensity diminishing. She was getting used to facing her feelings and found them less overwhelming over time.

Eventually, Lara shifted to the more challenging "present-moment exposure"—immediately after Jane made one of her remarks.

## • *Example*

Jane did it again—boasting this time about her sales numbers. I felt like calling her on it, but saying nasty things is schema coping. So I sat there at my desk and watched the feelings—anger, of course. And not being as good as her—that one is the worst. I could feel the knot in my stomach, and the urge was still there to call her "Madam Gloat," as I had done before.

But I just watched the feeling instead, describing to myself what it was like (a big angry fist). I had judgment thoughts, so I just said *judgment…judgment…judgment.* There were a lot of them.

Eventually I felt enough acceptance of the *I'm a failure feeling* that I knew I wasn't going to act on it. That's when I thought about my intention, which is to say something nice or affirming to Jane. After a while, I told her, "Good job with the sales," and more or less let it go.

•

The object of exposure is to reach that moment when you are *willing* to feel the schema emotions and still carry out your intentions. Lara, you'll notice, kept observing her "failure feeling" until she was ready to say something affirming to Jane. At the beginning, right after Jane's remark, Lara was tempted to launch into an attack (SCB). But instead of trying to avoid the emotion, Lara observed it. After a period of exposure, she felt enough acceptance to consider values-based alternatives.

---

# Exercise 12.2 Keeping an Exposure Record

As you expose yourself to schema emotions—first with images of past upsets, and later, present-moment situations—it can help you stay motivated if you keep a record of your progress. For each exposure you do, note the outcome on the following Exposure Record.

To fill out the record, identify the emotion you are experiencing and write it in the first column. Then use the second column to describe in a few words how you were triggered. Note whether the exposure was based on images of past situations and the accompanying emotions (imagery based, or IB) or based on present-moment (PM) experience, by putting an "X" in the appropriate column. In the "Outcome" column, you might note answers to any of the following:

- Did you feel more accepting and less avoidant as you observed the emotion?

- Did the impact or quality of the emotion change, or did the emotion morph into other emotions?

- Did you find yourself getting used to the emotion?

- For present-moment exposures, did you act on urges or use SCBs? Were you able to act on a values-based intention?

- Has anything changed in your relationship to the emotion? For example, do you feel less afraid of it or more comfortable with watching the emotional wave?

# Exposure Record

| Emotion | Trigger Situation | Exposure Type | | Outcome |
|---------|-------------------|:---:|:---:|---------|
| | | IB | PM | |
| | | | | |
| | | | | |
| | | | | |
| | | | | |
| | | | | |
| | | | | |
| | | | | |
| | | | | |
| | | | | |
| | | | | |

- *Example*

It's me, Lara, again. Over three weeks of doing exposures, here are my outcomes:

## Lara's Exposure Record

| Emotion | Trigger Situation | Exposure Type | | Outcome |
|---------|-------------------|-----|-----|---------|
| | | **IB** | **PM** | |
| Anger/failure feeling | Jane boasting how fast she is. | X | | No change in feeling; a little afraid of it. I see how driven I feel to attack her. |
| Anger/failure feeling | Jane pretending to commiserate when I made a mistake. | X | | No change in feeling. |
| Anger/failure feeling | Boyfriend criticized some clothes I bought. | X | | A little less upset; able to tolerate the feeling; learning to just watch it. |
| Hurt/rejected | Boyfriend late. | X | | Stayed with it longer and got a little more used to the feeling; accepted it more. |
| Anger/failure feeling | Jane brags how close she is to our boss. | X | | Upset went down during longer exposure; many judgments; more accepting of failure feeling; feeling changed to sadness. |
| Anger/failure feeling | Jane boasts about sales. | | X | Resisted SCB; was able to act on intention. |
| Failure feeling | Boss criticizes that I don't convert enough of my leads. | | X | SCB: Made excuses, which he didn't like. Rewrote my leads-conversion script (values-based behavior). Exposure didn't go well; avoided it; lost in self-judgment thoughts. |

| | | | | |
|---|---|---|---|---|
| Anger/feeling as if there's something wrong with me | Jane stands looking down at my desk as if she's judging me. | | X | Long exposure until more acceptance of feeling. Labeled judgments; no SCBs; asked Jane if she needed something; less afraid of feeling. |
| Failure feeling | Boyfriend angry. | X | | Exposed to feeling later; more accepting. |
| Hurt/rejected | Boyfriend cancels date. | | X | Tell him I'll call him back before getting into SCB. Long exposure until I feel less overwhelmed by hurt. In calm mood, make a new date. |

•

In Lara's record, she is exposing herself to more than one emotion (anger/failure and hurt/ rejection). This is common. Several different schema emotions are likely to show up in your record too. You may experience varying levels of success with each emotion. The main goals are to keep exposing yourself to your difficult emotions until you further develop acceptance and the ability to tolerate the feelings and to increasingly turn from SCBs toward values-based responses.

# CHAPTER 13

# Acceptance

Acceptance of your schema emotions depends, in part, on learning to have compassion for yourself as an emotional being. You have struggled with maladaptive schemas, and the pain they generate, since childhood. You have felt this pain many times and in many relationships. And you aren't alone. Almost everyone carries schema pain—the consequence of the inevitable wounds from growing up.

The fact that schema pain is the norm doesn't make it easy. But it also isn't something to be ashamed of. It's part of the struggle of being alive.

## Learning to Accept

The following acceptance and compassion meditation will help you (1) observe schema emotions without resistance, (2) accept them as a necessary part of living, and (3) strengthen compassion for yourself as someone who faces this pain.

---

## Exercise 13.1 Acceptance and Compassion Meditation

Record and play back this meditation, or have someone read it to you. Pause between sentences to allow time for them to sink in.

*Get comfortable in your chair and gently close your eyes. Begin by focusing your attention on your breathing for a few breaths.*

*Now recall a moment when one of your schemas was triggered in an important relationship. Maybe you felt deprived, abandoned, defective, or ashamed. Try to contact the core feeling in that moment when the schema was triggered. Where in your body do you experience that schema feeling?*

*Look back and try to recall how many times that feeling came up today. How many times over the past week? How many times over the past month? See if you can recall the very first time you had this feeling or one of the first times you had it.*

*Has this feeling been with you for a long time? Does it come up in many different relationships? Stay with this pain and breathe with it. If you notice any urges to escape in order to push away this experience, just notice that urge and see if you can allow yourself to stay with this experience. What does it feel like to fully experience this feeling without struggling? Can you allow yourself to feel 100 percent of your experiences with compassion and gentle kindness toward yourself? Can you make space for all the parts of your experience? Does this experience have to be pushed away or avoided? Or is this pain something you can handle—something you can observe nonjudgmentally and fully experience?*

*Notice any thoughts, emotions, sensations, and urges that are coming up or getting more intense, and just observe them all with kindness and willingness, as if this schema-related pain were a crying baby. See if you can allow yourself to invite this pain in and embrace it as a part of you, a part that has always been with you and always will be there. Nothing needs to be fixed; nothing has to be changed. You are exactly where you should be. When you are ready, gradually widen your attention and slowly open your eyes.*

---

## • *Example*

I'm Don, a sixty-year-old retired carpenter. I've struggled with defectiveness/shame and abandonment/instability schemas for as long as I can remember.

When I did the acceptance and compassion meditation, right away I was into those familiar feelings: shame, worthlessness, fear of being seen as bad, fear of being left by someone. I didn't try to stop them as I've done so many times. I just said to myself, *Okay, here they are. Just watch them.*

The part where you remember all the times you felt this way, back to the earliest days, really hit me. I have to say that I got emotional—sad—realizing how long these feelings have been inside me.

The part where you see your pain as a crying child made me feel as if I were that child—because I know how hard it's been. But—I was surprised—I also felt brave, as if I had dealt with a lot of pain in my life—not always well, but it kept coming at me.

So the meditation helped me see that I've been through a lot. I felt the truth of that—and that maybe I can now face this pain differently.

●

Don did the "Acceptance and Compassion Meditation" four times because, as he said, "I kept getting something out of it." We suggest that you repeat the meditation several times too. Many people have described a cumulative effect, where they experience a "softening" and increased openness to their feelings, as well as greater compassion for their struggles.

---

# Exercise 13.2 Facing Your Worst Self: Acceptance and Defusion

Now it's time to go beyond schema emotions. In this guided visualization, you'll vividly recall a time when schema coping strategies led to regrettable behavior. In essence, you're going back to a situation in which you were your "worst self" with others.

As you'll see in a moment, the purpose of this exercise isn't to push you into self-hating judgments. It's to see this painful moment from a distance, from the unchanging observer self who watches everything you do, every moment of your life. This self is the core "you," who can observe everything the *worst self* does and still not be the worst self.

Here's the script for the visualization. Record it with pauses between the sentences so that you can absorb the experience (based on Ciarrochi and Bailey 2008).

*Think back to a specific time when you were at your worst.… Imagine, as vividly as you can, being this "worst self."… Notice the feelings that push and pull at you. Notice how your "worst self" thinks. Let yourself be aware of specific thoughts.… See how your "worst self" behaves with others and how far this is from your values.*

*Now notice that within you is somebody looking at this "worst self." This is a self that watches your "worst self" and witnesses everything it experiences. This part of you is the observer self.*

*Even though your thoughts, feelings, urges, and sensations are continuously changing, there is still a consistent "you" throughout. There is a "you" that can watch all of your experiences without being those experiences or struggling with them. Just become aware of this person behind your eyes that watches your "worst self." Can you experience what it feels like to be the observer?*

*Now consider this: If you can observe your "worst self," then you are not the same as that "worst self." If you can observe the thoughts and feelings connected to your worst self, then you aren't equivalent to those thoughts and feelings. You are the observer.*

*Can you imagine that you are not your breathing and your body and its sensations, that you are not your emotions or your thoughts? Many parts of you have changed over the years. You have aged. Your appearance has changed. Your thoughts and feelings are constantly changing. But the observer self has always been there, never changing. See if you can sense this deeper "you." Think of yourself as being like the sky, being an unchanging perspective from which you notice and hold the ever-changing weather of your awareness.*

*Now notice all of the experiences that have shown up today—particularly the difficult thoughts and feelings of your "worst self." And as you do, notice that you're here now, watching all of it. See if you can make space to be the observer right now. You are exactly who you should be. Nothing needs to be changed. Nothing needs to be fixed.*

This visualization can change your relationship to everything you think and feel and do. It helps you observe thoughts and feelings from a safe, clear place—your core self. While you can't stop schema thoughts and feelings, you can watch these inner experiences with detached nonjudgment.

---

Looking back, the way you coped with schema thoughts and feelings may seem absurdly wrong. But the unchanging observer self sees it differently. It was a day like thousands of others, where you were coping with pain as best you could *at that moment*.

## • *Example*

The scene I chose happened when my daughter wanted to go to this late-night party. She was very determined, but it was way past the time she was supposed to be home. There was a lot of disrespect—let me put it that way—which hammers on my schemas. My inner reaction was: *If you don't respect me, then I'm nothing. I'm worthless.* It was so hard to feel that I tried to drown it out with rage. I screamed the most awful, unforgivable things at her. I'm ashamed to say what they were.

But this meditation where I watched myself changed something about that memory. I had always felt as if I were that person, that bad dad. Instead, I was the person who's observed my whole life, watching the loving, sweet things I've done; the pain I've felt; the joy I've felt (and I had this memory of when she was born), as well as things I so much regret—everything. I felt that terrible moment—my worst moment—with her in that context. I wish I'd never said those things, but I could watch it, just as I have watched my whole life.

●

# When You're Triggered, FACE

We're going to shift from practicing acceptance and defusion in remembered scenes to doing it in real life. When you're hit suddenly by schema emotions, we encourage you to use a response called "FACE," which is an acronym for:

1. Feel.

2. Accept.

3. Call thoughts a name.

4. Express intention.

These are all things you've practiced before, but now it's time to do them *as you are triggered*. The first step is to open yourself to the emotion. Running away has bruised your relationships. The best thing to do is observe the feeling and find words to describe it.

Next, accept this experience. A difficult emotion has shown up in your life, and it will run its course. It is weather that will exist for a while in your sky. Let this feeling be what it is. Make room for it.

As thoughts show up, give them a name: *I'm having a judgment thought…. I'm having a worry thought…. I'm having a failure thought…. I'm having a "why" thought* (trying to explain why things happen). Make up your own labels. And abbreviate the label if that feels better (*worry thought… bad thought*).

The last step of FACE is to express your intention. Based on your values, what actions have you committed to in this relationship? If you could be the person you want to be, what would you do *right now*? Then do it.

Notice how FACE gives you an opportunity to expose yourself to schema feelings and defuse from schema thoughts as they show up. We know this isn't easy, and there will be triggering situations where you fall back into old SCBs. One way to increase the likelihood of using FACE is to create reminders. Put a FACE sign up on your bathroom mirror, in your wallet, on your nightstand, or in your desk drawer at work. Let these reminders help you stay aware of your commitment to FACE.

We also suggest using 3 by 5 index cards to create FACE cards that look like this:

_____

F:

A:

C:

E:

Every time you have a triggering situation, fill out the FACE card as follows:

F:   (Name the feeling.)

A:   (Did you accept the feeling? yes/no)

C:   (Name the thoughts that came up.)

E:   (Name your intention in this relationship; did you do it? yes/no)

Your FACE cards will provide a record of your experiences and progress with dealing with schema triggers. But perhaps most important, keeping a FACE record will help you recognize the moment of choice when you can go either way—back to the SCBs or toward your relationship values.

## • *Example*

I decided to use FACE, initially, with situations that came up in this political action group I belong to. I find that people there frequently hurt me. The next time I was triggered, I actually used it. I watched the feelings (hurt, worthlessness) and thoughts (judgments, "why" thoughts). Then, instead of withdrawing, I acted on my intention to clarify the other person's motivation in saying what he or she said. I was pleased with myself, and then I promptly forgot to use FACE. I got triggered a number of times—once to the point where I flew out of a meeting and considered quitting.

Three weeks went by. I was about to visit my dad, and I thought about FACE again. The man drives me nuts—opinionated, full of advice, critical. This time I decided to use the FACE card. Here's the first one I filled out:

---

**Political Action Group**

F: *Hurt, worthless, angry.*

A: *Yes—I stayed with it, just watching.*

C: *Judgment thoughts—lots of them.*

E: *Yes—Decided to be more honest; told him I was hurt.*

---

I filled out four FACE cards in the two days when I was visiting, and I found that they helped me keep my intention. I also found—and this was a surprise—that when I told my dad I was hurt, he backed off and was kinder.

●

As we're sure you are finding, acceptance of schema-driven emotions isn't easy. But with practice and commitment, you can do it. Using the FACE process, you can learn to observe painful feelings and thoughts, rather than getting swept away by them. Your reward will be strong, enduring relationships—connections you can count on.

# CHAPTER 14

# Nonviolent Communication

Conflict is a major trigger for schema pain, and it frequently results in aggressive or hostile SCBs. One way to protect your relationships from schema-driven anger is to learn the skill of nonviolent communication. You can still say everything you need to, but without the damage wrought by verbal aggression.

Nonviolent communication has these qualities (Rosenberg 2003):

- It is nonattacking and nonblaming.

- It doesn't threaten.

- It is couched in preferences and needs, rather than demands.

- It allows room for the other person's feelings, preferences, and needs.

When a conflict arises, two types of nonviolent communication may be useful: limit setting and assertive requests. *Limit setting* expresses that something needs to stop. Essentially, it is saying no. *Assertive requests* convey, in a nonattacking way, a personal need.

# Limit Setting

There are two steps to nonviolent limit setting: (1) validate the other person's preference or desire, and (2) express a clear, specific limit. For example, "I appreciate how much you enjoy a good steak (validating), but bistro food would be too heavy for me tonight (limit setting)."

Notice that the other person isn't blamed for his or her preferences ("Haven't you clogged your arteries enough for one week?"). The limit is expressed clearly and assertively, leaving little room for debate.

Here's another example: "I know you're tired and frustrated (validation), but I have to ask that we remain civil (limit setting)."

The speaker appreciates the plight of the other person, but sends a clear, nonblaming message about how he or she expects to be treated.

And here's a final example: "I appreciate how much fun you're having, and how you'd like to stay and keep partying (validation), but I've got an early morning and I have to get to bed (assertive request)."

While limit setting allows other people to want what they want, it also expresses needs in a way that no one can deny. After all, who could argue that you don't need sleep or that you should like being yelled at? Who would suggest that if you aren't hungry, you should eat a big meal anyway?

---

## Exercise 14.1 Set Your Own Limits

For each of the following three situations, write your own limit-setting script:

1.  Your ten-year-old daughter is getting three to four hours of homework a night. She is feeling overwhelmed, and you have found her crying. In a conference, her teacher emphasizes the importance of discipline for success. You decide to set a limit regarding this teacher's demands. What would you say?

Validation: _____

_____

Assertive Limit: _____

_____

*Example response:* "I appreciate your teaching the value of discipline and hard work. However, I prefer that my daughter do no more than two hours of homework per night so that she has time for play."

2.  Your partner wants to invite someone for the weekend whom you find odious. They are good friends, but you don't want this person in your house. What would you say?

Validation: _____

_____

Assertive Limit: _____

_____

*Example response:* "I know you really enjoy each other, and it would be a chance to spend some time together. Honestly, it would make my weekend too uncomfortable if he were in the house."

3.  You're in the fifteen-item-and-under line at the supermarket. Someone in front of you has an overflowing cart—way over the limit.

Validation: _____

_____

Assertive Limit: _____

_____

*Example response:* "I'm sure you're pressed for time and trying to get out of here. This is the line for fifteen items, and I'd appreciate it if you'd use one of the lines that could accommodate a full cart."

# Assertive Requests

There are four steps to making an assertive request: (1) describe the problem in nonblaming language, (2) describe your feelings, (3) express your need as a value, and (4) make one specific behavioral request.

When you describe the problem, stick to the facts. Say exactly what's happened or not happened, using objective language. Avoid using judgments or expressing opinions about the other person's behavior.

Try not to use sentences that start with "You…": "*You're* always late," "*You* never consider my needs," "*You're* too critical." Instead describe factually and accurately the issue: "When I hurt my hand, you said I wasn't being careful enough."

Express how the problem has affected you emotionally: "I felt sad," "I felt alone," "I felt hurt," "I felt helpless and frustrated." Avoid using your feelings to blame the other person: "You *made me* feel sad." Also make sure you don't express judgments disguised as feelings: "I feel that you don't care." The phrase "I feel that…" is always a tip-off that you're expressing an opinion rather than emotion.

Describe your need in terms of a relationship value. For example, "I need connection, honesty, fairness, respect, caring," and so on. Assertive requests always end with asking for a specific behavioral change. Don't ask the other person to change his or her attitude or feelings—that isn't possible. Instead, describe exactly what you would like the person to *do* differently.

---

# Exercise 14.2 Make a Request

For each of the following situations, write out the four components of an assertive request. Essentially you are creating a script. This is something you can do whenever you need to carefully plan a request (particularly in situations where you or the other person has gotten angry in the past).

1. You are hosting a potluck family gathering. Your sister always seems to have an excuse for why she doesn't bring anything. The last time, she claimed an electricity failure prevented her from cooking. You feel irritated, but mostly hurt, that she puts no effort into family events. You'd like her, out of respect, to bring something—even if she can't prepare what she promised.

   The problem: _____

   _____

   Your feeling: _____

   _____

   Your need: _____

Your request: _____

_____

*Example request:* "For the last few gatherings, you weren't able to bring anything for the potluck. To be truthful, I felt a little hurt that you didn't find a way to bring something, and I need to feel that there is mutual respect in our relationship. Even if what you plan to bring doesn't work out, could you bring some contribution to the party?"

2. Your boss assigns staggered lunch breaks, and you *always* get the last break: one to two o'clock. You feel frustrated and unimportant in terms of the lunch arrangements—and often hungry. Out of fairness, you would like the lunch breaks to rotate.

The problem: _____

_____

Your feeling: _____

_____

Your need: _____

_____

Your request: _____

_____

*Example request:* "Currently I get the last lunch break. I feel frustrated, because I'm often hungry by that time. I'm hoping for a fairer system; could we rotate lunch breaks?"

*Note:* Expressing that you feel unimportant—even though it's true—might be too much disclosure in a work setting.

3. Over the past several weeks, your partner has seemed withdrawn and unhappy. But when you ask, your partner either denies having a problem or resists talking about it. The withdrawal has left you feeling hurt and alone. Honesty and closeness really matter to you in this relationship, and you need your partner to open up and tell you what's going on.

The problem: _____

Your feeling: _____

_____

Your need: _____

_____

Your request: _____

_____

*Example request:* "Something has changed recently: you seem sad and withdrawn, but you won't tell me what's going on. I'm feeling very alone right now and hurt, because you seem so far away. I need our relationship to have the honesty and closeness that makes it wonderful. What has happened? I need to know."

---

## • *Example*

I'm Juliet, a thirty-eight-year-old teacher. I'm going on a retreat with the rest of the faculty in my charter high school. These people should all join "Backbiters Anonymous." There are so many nasty remarks—I don't want to hear them; I don't want to encourage them. Honestly, I dread going.

The other problem with the retreat is that we're supposed to come up with ideas to improve the school. I do have ideas—several of them—but these two pompous science teachers always drown me out. Then I get angry, and they put me down for losing it. I get so upset with the backbiting and being ignored that I sit there seething the whole time.

So I did the exercise on nonviolent communication and decided to use this stuff at the retreat. First, I wanted to set limits about the backbiting, and so I planned out what to say:

"I know that a lot of annoying things happen at school (validation), but I don't want to get into complaining about stuff people do or criticizing them (request)."

Then I wrote out scripts for several requests to make policy changes. Here's one of them:

"Right now there are only three minutes between periods. Kids don't have enough time to go to their lockers and get to the next class. They keep arriving late and disrupting the first part of every class (problem). When they arrive late, I feel frustrated and anxious that we're losing time (feeling). I need for my classes to be conducive to learning and not starting with chaos all the time (need). Could we agree to increase the break between periods to five minutes (request)?"

I had to edit these scripts to get rid of the blame. I'm so angry about things at school that judgments tend to leak in. But I got the attacking stuff out, and I was surprised that several people agreed that we should stop criticizing one another, and one of my policy ideas got accepted.

I'm working on using nonviolent communication in everyday situations where I'm triggered. Saying things without blame or judgment is an important change I'm trying to make.

●

# CHAPTER 15

# Defusion, Acceptance, and Values in Everyday Life

This chapter will focus on integrating all of the skills that you have learned in this book and incorporating them into your daily life. Exercise 15.1 initially will illustrate the ways in which your schema thoughts and feelings can act as barriers to specific values-based actions. The second part of the exercise will help you practice acceptance of your schema pain in order to build willingness to have it so that it doesn't stand in the way of valued behaviors. This second part of the exercise will incorporate defusion and acceptance to assist you in actualizing your values in everyday life. Every step that we take toward doing what is really important to us in relationships will inevitably bring up our schema pain; therefore it is extremely important to build willingness and acceptance to have our pain in order to prevent it from stopping us from behaving in ways that are consistent with our values.

Exercise 15.2 will help you generate a key-person action plan in a particular relationship. The purpose of generating a key-person action plan is to identify the schemas that get triggered for you with different people, to practice identifying the moment of choice to behave differently, to identify alternative behaviors, and to be able to differentiate between old behaviors and values-based behaviors. When trying out new behaviors, ask yourself if you are doing the behavior in order to move toward being the kind of person you want to be or in order to escape schema pain. The key-person action plan will help you identify and practice new behaviors in your daily life and assess the outcomes of your new chosen behaviors.

---

# Exercise 15.1 The Flip Side

It's important to recognize how avoiding the thoughts and feelings connected to your schemas affects your values and behaviors. This exercise will help you identify some of the costs of avoiding your schema pain and encourage you to build willingness to stay in contact with it (based on Eifert and Forsyth 2005).

Begin by getting out a piece of paper and thinking about a schema that has greatly affected your relationships. Think about the thoughts and feelings connected to this schema; what do you believe about yourself in relationships? What is a catastrophic or terrible thought that you have about yourself and sometimes get fused with? Write down these thoughts on the piece of paper. For example, if you have a defectiveness/shame schema, you might write down "No one will ever understand me," "If anyone ever really knew me, they would leave me," "I should never share my insecurities with other people," or "I'm too disgusting to be loved."

Underneath these thoughts, write down some feelings that are connected to this schema, such as "shame, anxiety, fear, hopelessness."

Now as you read these thoughts and feelings, ask yourself, *Have any of these thoughts and feelings ever stopped me from doing something that was very important to me?* Now flip the paper over, and on the other side of the paper, write down what these thoughts have stopped you from doing. For example, you might write down that these thoughts have stopped you from sharing your anxiety about work with your partner or sharing some other vulnerability with a friend, or maybe these thoughts have stopped you from expressing resentment to a friend or from being honest with a family member. Ask yourself if this important thing that you have stopped yourself from doing is connected to any of your values. Maybe you value being honest, open, vulnerable, expressive, or assertive. What values are connected to this important action? Write down all the values underneath this action.

- ## *Example*

Hi, it's Mark. Here's what the front of my paper looked like:

"I'm too disgusting for anyone to love me. Anxiety, fear, hopelessness, shame."

The back of my paper looked like this:

"I don't share with Tracy when I feel hurt by something she's done. This is connected to my value of being honest and genuine with her."

•

Now, turn the paper over and look at all your schema thoughts and feelings. Bring this piece of paper up close to your face, as close to your face as you can while still being able to read it. Take a look at it; what comes up as you read these things? Are any of the emotions coming up right now? Are any urges coming up? Do you have an urge to look away, or to get the paper farther away from you? How do you usually relate to these thoughts and feelings when they come up? Do you look at them, and are you curious and open to them; or do you try to push them away? If your urge is to look away or push the piece of paper away, try acting on that urge by looking away, trying to avoid it, or even trying to throw the paper far away from you. Have you ever managed to permanently keep these thoughts and feelings far away? Have you ever been able to permanently remove any of these thoughts from your mind?

When you push these thoughts and feelings away from you, notice what else is farther away from you. What is on the back of that paper? The farther away these thoughts and feelings are, the farther away your values are and the farther away your valued behavior is. The closer your schema pain is, and the thoughts and feelings that come up with it, the closer you are to your values. Would you be willing to have these thoughts and feelings that are connected to your schema and to stay in contact with them, if doing so would bring you closer to being the kind of person you want to be?

## The Flip-Side Meditation

If you are willing to stay in contact with this experience, let's look at some of these thoughts on the paper. How many words are in each sentence you wrote? How many letters are in each sentence? What is the color of the ink that you used? Try to read the sentences backward. Would you be willing to have these thoughts, to just notice them and stay in contact with them, but not buy into them? Bring them closer to you; hold them lightly in your hands. They are just words on paper, not facts; they are not real physical barriers to your valued action. They don't have to stop you from being how you want to be in the world and taking action in your life. Would you be willing to have these thoughts come up more often if it would bring you closer to being the kind of person you want to be? Do you think it would be possible to take steps toward the action on the back of this paper without having these thoughts and feelings come up? If your answer is no, continue contacting this experience to come closer to these feelings so that these thoughts and feelings won't have the power to stop you from doing important things in your life.

## The Flip-Side Visualization

If you are willing to go toward this schema pain and get curious about what it really feels like, begin by closing your eyes.

*Stay mindful of your breathing, and think about the action that this pain has stopped you from taking and the values connected to this action. Imagine doing the valued behavior you wrote down on the paper. Visualize the scene. Notice how your schema pain increases as you imagine taking this action, and stay in contact with it. Are the feelings that you wrote on the paper coming up for you right now, as you imagine taking this step toward your value? Do these feelings have to be your enemy, or are they something that you can have, experience, and hold? The more you are willing to have your schema pain, the less that pain will be an obstacle to your values. Are you willing to get closer and contact this pain if it means that it will bring you closer to taking action toward your values and to being the kind of person you want to be?*

*Notice where in your body this painful feeling is. What shape does it have? What does this emotion feel like in your body right at this moment? What color is it? How big is it? How heavy is this feeling in your body? How often has this feeling come up for you this week, this month? Can you remember one of the very first times you experienced this feeling in your body? Can you get very curious about this experience that has been with you for so long and that you've been struggling against so much? Are you willing to experience this schema pain 100 percent, as it is right now?*

*Are you willing to have this experience come up this week and take this step toward your values? If your answer is yes, pick a specific day to act on this intention; carry this paper with you and take a look at it right before you take this step, and remind yourself that you are willing to bring this experience with you toward your valued intention.*

# Exercise 15.2 Creating an Action Plan

Now that you have built the willingness to have the schema pain that will show up when you are taking steps toward your values, the next step is to clarify specific alternative responses to replace old schema coping behaviors. The following section will focus on identifying key responses to use with specific people in your life. You will begin by identifying the old schema coping behaviors that you use when your schema is triggered, and then you will identify alternative responses based on your values.

Finally, once you have committed to trying out your alternative, values-based behavior, it's essential to remain mindful of its outcome in your relationship and to be aware of how it affects the other person. It's important to make the commitment to not just try out the new behavior, but also notice its short-term and long-term consequences. What is the other person's reaction? What does the other person's face look like when you do the new behavior? What is the person's response? Did it make your relationship closer or more distant? Did it bring you closer to being the kind of person you want to be in the relationship? Will this new behavior benefit the relationship in the long run? In what ways? In what ways might you modify the behavior to be more effective the next time you try it?

Asking yourself these questions will help you distinguish whether a behavior is a new behavior based on values or just another version of an old schema coping behavior. (For example: you may, at times, respond to an emotional deprivation schema by becoming more demanding or, at other times, by giving in and accommodating. Both are strategies to avoid the thoughts and feelings connected to the emotional deprivation schema.) After trying out the new behavior you identified in your action plan, look back at these questions and assess whether this behavior is a new behavior that is based on your values or an old schema coping behavior that is functioning to avoid pain.

# Key-Person Action Plan

Other Person's Name: _____

1.  What is one schema that often is triggered for you in this relationship?

    _____

    _____

    _____

2.  What situations trigger this schema in this relationship? (For example, "Making decisions," "Asserting myself," "Moments when I feel criticized," "When this person expresses a negative emotion or hurt feelings," "When this person is unavailable.")

    _____

    _____

    _____

    _____

3.  What specific thoughts come up when this schema gets triggered in this relationship? These thoughts may include future predicting stories, feared expectations of outcomes, rules about behavior, or negative stories about yourself or about the other person; for example, "If I express my hurt feelings, this person will leave me, distance himself or herself, or retaliate against me"; "There's something wrong with me"; "I should be able to assert myself"; "I can't trust this person"; "I'm too much to handle"; "My sharing too much will scare this person away"; "If I say no, this person will feel hurt and disappointed by me."

    _____

    _____

    _____

4.  What sensations come up when this schema gets triggered in this relationship? (For example, "Heart pounding, lump in throat, heaviness in my chest, feeling suffocated, tightness in my stomach.")

    _____

    _____

    _____

    _____

5.  What feelings come up when this schema is triggered in this relationship? (For example, "Hopelessness, fear, shame, guilt, anger, deprivation, guilty, powerless.")

    _____

    _____

    _____

    _____

6.  What schema coping behaviors do you use in this relationship? (What do you usually do when you get triggered in this relationship? For example, "Run away, yell, explain, blame, accuse, justify myself, demand, criticize, subjugate, give up, surrender, accommodate.")

    _____

    _____

    _____

    _____

7.  What are your specific values in this relationship? What kind of person do you want to be in this relationship, regardless of the outcome? (For example, "I want to be assertive, honest, collaborative, patient, accepting, self-sufficient, forgiving, compassionate, grateful.")

    _____

    _____

    _____

    _____

8.   How important are these values to you (on a scale from 1 to 10)? _____

9.   Based on your values, what is an alternative behavior that you can do instead?

_____

_____

_____

_____

10.   At what moments will you practice this new behavior? To identify the moment of choice to behave differently, recall a time when you used these schema coping behaviors in this relationship and regretted your behaviors. Notice the scene; what was the exact moment when you got triggered? What did the other person say or do? As you notice your reaction, try to be aware of what came first as soon as you got triggered—was it a thought, a feeling, a sensation, or an urge? What came next? Write them down. What can you do in the moment to remind yourself that this particular thought, feeling, sensation, or urge is connected to your schemas and will take you farther away from your values if you act on it? What can you do in the moment to remind yourself of the consequences of acting on that particular thought, urge, feeling, or sensation? Identify a specific moment in the scene where you had a choice to behave differently and not make things worse (for example, "When I start feeling suffocated, I will remind myself that this is a moment of choice to behave differently and that it's a sign that my self-sacrifice/ subjugation schema is triggered," "When I have an urge to run away, it's related to my fear of being abandoned, and it's a moment of choice to behave differently," or "When I feel guilty, it's an opportunity to be mindful and curious about how I could behave differently").

_____

_____

_____

_____

- ## *Example*

My name is Marlena. This is the Key-Person Action Plan that I wrote to deal with Adam, my boyfriend.

# Key-Person Action Plan

Other Person's Name:  <u>Adam</u>

1.  What is one schema that often is triggered for you in this relationship?

    *Emotional deprivation*

2.  What situations trigger this schema in this relationship?

    *My emotional deprivation schema gets triggered when Adam is busy, when he says no to a request of mine, when I feel misunderstood, and when he doesn't follow through with plans.*

3.  What specific thoughts come up when this schema is triggered in this relationship?

    *He will never understand me; I'm always going to feel alone in this relationship; He is selfish; I need to leave this relationship; This is unfair; I shouldn't allow him to treat me like this; My needs will never get met in this relationship.*

4.  What sensations come up when this schema gets triggered in this relationship?

    *Tightness in throat, heart pounding, breathing feels shallow, stabbing feeling in my stomach.*

5.  What feelings come up when this schema is triggered?

    *Loneliness, despair, shame, fear*

6.  What schema coping behaviors do you use in this relationship?

    *I demand that he listen, and I try to get him to understand me. I give ultimatums. I explain myself and how I feel. I blame him and accuse him of mistreating me.*

7.   What are your specific values in this relationship? What kind of person do you want to be in this relationship, regardless of the outcome?

*Appreciative, accepting, and flexible.*

8.   How important are these values to you (on a scale from 1 to 10)?  __9__

9.   Based on your values, what is an alternative behavior that you can do instead?

*Express my feelings and needs instead of criticizing and blaming. Let him know I want to feel close to him when I feel hurt. Express appreciation for him.*

10.   At what moments will you practice this new behavior? To identify the moment of choice to behave differently, recall a time when you used these schema coping behaviors in this relationship and regretted your behaviors. Notice the scene; what was the exact moment when you got triggered? What did the other person say or do? As you notice your reaction, try to be aware of what came first as soon as you got triggered—was it a thought, a feeling, a sensation, or an urge? What came next? Write them down. What can you do in the moment to remind yourself that this particular thought, feeling, sensation, or urge is connected to your schemas and will take you farther away from your values if you act on it? What can you do in the moment to remind yourself of the consequences of acting on that triggered thought, urge, feeling, or sensation? Identify a specific moment in the scene where you had a choice to behave differently and not make things worse.

*When I feel the loneliness come up or when I feel the stabbing feeling in my stomach, I have a choice to behave differently. When I have the thought that he will never understand me, it's a story connected to my emotional deprivation schema and I have a choice to behave differently.*

●

Although you've finished working through this book, your work is not done. It has just started, because the most important part of learning these skills is using them in your everyday life. Changing your relationships and the way they are currently functioning requires a commitment to practicing these skills on a daily basis, as well as noticing every moment of action as an opportunity to move closer to or farther away from the kind of person you want to be and to build the kind of relationships you want to have. Now, your work is to practice and notice your schemas when they are triggered, notice the predictions and stories connected to your schemas and your impulses to act on them, stay mindful and compassionate with your schema pain, and remember that you still have the choice to act on your values. You've learned a lot of new skills, and the more you apply them and practice them in everyday life, the more effective you will be and the more gratifying your relationships will be.

The area where the most pain comes up for all human beings is within relationships. Relationships are risky and scary; everyone is afraid of being rejected or abandoned. All people yearn for connection and belonging; therefore relationships inevitably bring up our deepest pain, fears, and insecurities, but they also provide us with the most joy, meaning, and fulfillment in life. Do we want to keep struggling with this unavoidable pain, or do we want to be able to move forward with this pain? To build satisfying relationships, we must be willing to cope with our pain in a way that doesn't damage and hurt our relationships. In essence this means noticing the painful thoughts and feelings that come up when our schemas are triggered and still taking steps in the direction of doing what matters.

# Appendix: Note to Therapists

This book is based on research conducted by Avigail Lev (2011). A randomized controlled trial of a ten-week ACT protocol showed significant decreases (Cohen's $D = 1.23$) in problematic interpersonal behaviors on the Inventory of Interpersonal Problems (IIP-64). Interpersonal problems are pervasive in the population seeking therapy and the majority of clients presenting with depression, anxiety, trauma, and Axis II disorders report problems in one or more significant relationships. Yet for all the pain these problems create, few systems of psychotherapy directly target the interpersonal behavior driving them, and research addressing what treatments effectively change disordered interpersonal functioning is inconsistent. Treatments fail either to target maladaptive coping behaviors, or to address underlying (transdiagnostic) causes of interpersonal problems, or to provide specific techniques for tolerating interpersonal distress. Inventories that adequately measure interpersonal behaviors are currently scarce. Therefore, while there are many treatments for interpersonal problems, evidence regarding their effectiveness in changing client behaviors in relationships and how they impact client interpersonal responses is mixed. This book offers a new treatment for chronic interpersonal problems, one that both targets the underlying factors driving maladaptive interpersonal behaviors and has research support.

# References

Ciarrochi, J., and A. Bailey. 2008. *A CBT Practitioner's Guide to ACT: How to Bridge the Gap Between Cognitive Behavioral Therapy and Acceptance and Commitment Therapy*. Oakland, CA: New Harbinger Publications.

Eifert, G.H., and J.P. Forsyth. 2005. *Acceptance & Commitment Therapy for Anxiety Disorders: A Practitioner's Treatment Guide to Using Mindfulness, Acceptance, and Values-Based Behavior Change Strategies*. Oakland, CA: New Harbinger Publications.

Forsyth, J.P., and G.H. Eifert. 2007. *The Mindfulness and Acceptance Workbook for Anxiety: A Guide to Breaking Free from Anxiety, Phobias, and Worry Using Acceptance and Commitment Therapy*. Oakland, CA: New Harbinger Publications.

Harris, R. 2009. *ACT Made Simple: An Easy-to-Read Primer on Acceptance and Commitment Therapy*. Oakland, CA: New Harbinger Publications.

Hayes, S. C. 2005. *Get Out of Your Mind and Into Your Life: The New Acceptance and Commitment Therapy*. With S. Smith. Oakland, CA: New Harbinger Publications.

Hayes, S. C., K. D. Strosahl, and K. G. Wilson. 1999. *Acceptance and Commitment Therapy: An Experiential Approach to Behavior Change*. New York: The Guilford Press.

Lev, A. 2011. "A New Group Therapy Protocol Combining Acceptance and Commitment Therapy (ACT) and Schema Therapy in the Treatment of Interpersonal Disorders: A Randomized Controlled Trial." PsyD diss., Wright Institute, Berkeley, CA.

Linehan, M. M. 1993. *Cognitive-Behavioral Treatment of Borderline Personality Disorder*. New York: The Guilford Press.

McKay, M., M. Davis, and P. Fanning. 2011. *Thoughts and Feelings: Taking Control of Your Moods and Your Life*. 4th ed. Oakland, CA: New Harbinger Publications.

McKay, M., and P. Fanning. 1991. *Prisoners of Belief: Exposing and Changing Beliefs That Control Your Life*. Oakland, CA: New Harbinger Publications.

McKay, M., A. Lev, and M. Skeen. 2012. *Acceptance and Commitment Therapy for Interpersonal Problems: Using Mindfulness, Acceptance, and Schema Awareness to Change Interpersonal Behaviors*. Oakland, CA: New Harbinger Publications.

Rosenberg, M. B. 2003. *Nonviolent Communication: A Language of Life*. Encinitas, CA: PuddleDancer Press.

Tavris, C. 1989. *Anger: The Misunderstood Emotion*. Rev. ed. New York: Touchstone.

Titchener, E. B. 1910. *Text-Book of Psychology*. New York: The MacMillan Company.

Vuille, P. 2006. Online forum comment, http://contextualscience.org/thoughts_as_sales_repre-sentatives, March 5, 9:49 a.m.

Young, J.E., J.S. Klosko, and M.E. Weishaar (2006). *Schema Therapy: A Practitioner's Guide*. New York: Guilford Press.

Young, J.E. (1999). *Cognitive Therapy for Personality Disorders: A Schema-Focused Approach*. Sarasota, FL: Professional Resource Exchange.

**Matthew McKay, PhD**, is a professor at the Wright Institute in Berkeley, CA. He has authored and coauthored numerous books, including The Relaxation and Stress Reduction Workbook, Self-Esteem, Thoughts and Feelings, When Anger Hurts, and ACT on Life Not on Anger. McKay received his PhD in clinical psychology from the California School of Professional Psychology, and specializes in the cognitive behavioral treatment of anxiety and depression. He lives and works in the Bay Area.

**Patrick Fanning** is a professional writer in the mental health field. He is author of Visualization for Change and Lifetime Weight Control and coauthor of several self-help books, including Self-Esteem and 50 Ways to Simplify Your Life.

**Avigail Lev, PsyD**, maintains a private practice in Berkeley, CA. She specializes in couples' therapy and also treats individuals who struggle with interpersonal problems, anxiety, trauma, chronic pain, and mood disorders. She has provided supervision, trainings, and workshops utilizing cognitive behavioral therapy (CBT) and is the coauthor of Acceptance and Commitment Therapy for Interpersonal Problems.

**Michelle Skeen, PsyD**, is a therapist who lives and works in San Francisco, CA. She has provided brief and long-term therapy for individuals and couples utilizing schema, cognitive, and behavioral therapies to address interpersonal issues, weight management, anger, depression, anxiety, disabilities, and trauma. She is the author of The Critical Partner and coauthor of Acceptance and Commitment Therapy for Interpersonal Problems, and is currently working on her fourth book for New Harbinger Publications, Love Me Don't Leave Me, a self-help book that provides breakthrough, evidence-based solutions for women (and men) struggling with the fear of abandonment. Michelle hosts a weekly radio show called Relationships 2.0 with Dr. Michelle Skeen on KCAA1050AM. To find out more about Michelle, visit her website at www.michelleskeen.com.

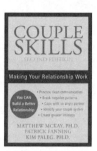

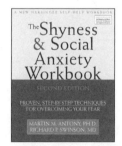

## FROM OUR PUBLISHER—

As the publisher at New Harbinger and a clinical psychologist since 1978, I know that emotional problems are best helped with evidence-based therapies. These are the treatments derived from scientific research (randomized controlled trials) that show what works. Whether these treatments are delivered by trained clinicians or found in a self-help book, they are designed to provide you with proven strategies to overcome your problem.

Therapies that aren't evidence-based—whether offered by clinicians or in books—are much less likely to help. In fact, therapies that aren't guided by science may not help you at all. That's why this New Harbinger book is based on scientific evidence that the treatment can relieve emotional pain.

This is important: if this book isn't enough, and you need the help of a skilled therapist, use the following resources to find a clinician trained in the evidence-based protocols appropriate for your problem. And if you need more support—a community that understands what you're going through and can show you ways to cope—resources for that are provided below, as well.

Real help is available for the problems you have been struggling with. The skills you can learn from evidence-based therapies will change your life.

Matthew McKay, PhD
Publisher, New Harbinger Publications

**new harbinger**
CELEBRATING
**40** YEARS

**If you need a therapist, the following organization can help you find a therapist trained in acceptance and commitment therapy (ACT).**

Association for Contextual Behavioral Science (ACBS)

**Please visit www.contextualscience.org
and click on *Find an ACT Therapist*.**

# Real change *is* possible

For more than forty-five years, New Harbinger has published proven-effective self-help books and pioneering workbooks to help readers of all ages and backgrounds improve mental health and well-being, and achieve lasting personal growth. In addition, our spirituality books offer profound guidance for deepening awareness and cultivating healing, self-discovery, and fulfillment.

Founded by psychologist Matthew McKay and Patrick Fanning, New Harbinger is proud to be an independent, employee-owned company. Our books reflect our core values of integrity, innovation, commitment, sustainability, compassion, and trust. Written by leaders in the field and recommended by therapists worldwide, New Harbinger books are practical, accessible, and provide real tools for real change.

**newharbingerpublications**